Plant Based Recipes for Dogs

Feed your dog for health & longevity

A Nutritional Lifestyle Guide

First Edition

HEATHER COSTER

This book is not meant to replace your veterinarian for specific health ailments. The author will not be held responsible for any adverse reactions recommended in this guide or illness arising from a failure by a reader to seek medical advice that may warrant expert health management.

Plant Based Recipes for Dogs
ISBN: 9781514100370

'Veganism is sustaining our future generations.'

In the memory of Brillo
The most gentle and kind dog; I miss you with every beat of my heart.

Sweet Potato Heart Treats

Testament to veganism for dogs; what people are saying around the world.

Remember that conventional pet food is pretty much junk food for your animals. It's full of animal by-products (intestines, bones, brains, etc.), preservatives, chemicals, and fillers. Personally I can't justify killing one animal to save or feed another. If you feed meat to your dogs, that's what we are doing…deciding that one life is more worthy than the other - **Alicia Silverstone, Actress and Vegan Author.**

A properly formulated vegan diet may be more healthy than many of the most popular and common commercial diets available - **James O'Hare, Canine Psychologist**

All of my beloved rescue dogs throughout the years have thrived on a vegan diet, in fact I have never had any that refused or did not enjoy the plant based foods. They have always been very healthy, strong and happy – **Pam Lightfoot, Veteran Vegan Advocate.**

Dogs can be healthy and in fact, thrive on a vegetarian or vegan diet - **Dr. Armaiti May, D.V.M., C.V.A.**

I fed dogs in my care vegan because `in my opinion it is not the prerogative of humans to decide which animals live and which die for dog food. I evolved a vegan dog food to circumvent this and to provide proper balanced nutrition for dogs, of premium quality to build and maintain health. Commercial non vegan food can shorten animal lives, be it the consumer, animal or obviously the consumed. Vegan dog food is better for dogs, the planet and carers; it's a win/win situation and a no brainer - **Anne Heritage, author of 'Bramble; the dog that wanted to live forever'**.

There is little doubt that a carefully balanced diet that does not contain meat can meet the nutritional requirements of the dog - **Animal Science, School of Environmental and Rural Science, University of New England.**

Studies and numerous case reports have shown that nutritionally sound vegetarian companion animal diets appear to be associated with the following health benefits: increased overall health and vitality, decreased incidences of cancer, infections, ectoparasites (fleas, ticks, lice and mites), improved coat condition, arthritis regression and diabetes regression - **Harbingers of a New Age**

My 36 Years of Experience Proves that DOGS CAN EAT VEGAN! The rescued dogs I've shared life with have all made remarkable transformations eating a 100% vegan diet, both in physical health and in temperament. For the committed vegan, it's the way to ensure your dog's health without intentionally harming other animals to do so - **Butterflies Katz, Author of The Vegan Truth**

CONTENTS

PREFACE.....1

VEGANISM AND ANIMAL RIGHTS.....3

WHY VEGANISM FOR DOGS?.....5

HEALTH AND NUTRITION FOR VEGAN DOGS.....8

COMMERCIAL PET FOODS | THE TRUTH.....13

THE PROTEIN MYTH | PLANT AND ANIMAL PROTEIN SOURCES. 16

A GUIDE TO GOODNESS IN NATURAL FOOD.....18

INGREDIENTS TO AVOID.....20

MAKING THE ADJUSTMENTS.....22

FEEDING GUIDELINES.....24

HOW TO COOK THE BASICS.....27

BREAKFAST RECIPES.....40

DINNER RECIPES.....47

DOG TREAT RECIPES.....71

FAST FOOD IDEAS.....100

KONG® FILLED TREAT IDEAS.....101

HOMEMADE REMEDIES.....102

INGREDIENTS & THEIR NUTRITIONAL VALUES.....104

SUPPLEMENTS.....130

VITAMIN, MINERAL AND MICRO MINERAL TABLE.....133

WAYS TO HELP YOUR DOG ACHIEVE LONGEVITY.....140

ABOUT THE AUTHOR.....144

RESOURCES.....146

PREFACE

If you are reading this book then you may well be an animal lover and perhaps a vegan yourself. You may be looking for inspiration on how and why some of us find feeding our canine friends a plant based diet is not just for health reasons, but morally and ethically it just feels right. You may just be curious about finding out how to incorporate plant based recipes into your dog's current meals. Or perhaps you already feed your dog a plant based lifestyle and are looking for new recipe ideas. Whoever you are and whatever lifestyle you choose, I salute you for reading this book because it may well change your views and opinions on the topics that many people find so controversial. The basis of this first edition is to provide more information, recipe ideas and also to highlight the common questions that I am asked when I dare to mention that my dogs live on a plant based diet! The general perception of feeding a vegan lifestyle to our pets is one of shock and horror. Many say how 'cruel' it is not to allow my dogs their heritage right to eat meat. And then there is the health question, some say, 'so what do you feed your dog? or 'how do they get their protein? They must be very 'hungry'! This is normally the staunch view of a meat eating human. I will touch on all the sensitive topics just because I think it is important to state why a plant based lifestyle is suitable for humans and dogs alike. Whilst this book is based around my own research, opinions and findings over the years working in animal welfare as a canine psychologist, the ultimate decision is down to you, the guardian, and what you choose to feed your canine friend. In my opinion the only way to make sure that our dogs get the right balance of nutrients is to make all meals from scratch using fresh organic ingredients. Many people love preparing home-made meals for their pets, but it does require a little time and effort on your behalf. It is certainly easier and quicker to open a can or a bag of dog food, but I find it incredibly rewarding and satisfying making and preparing meals and treats for my dogs, whilst being happy in the knowledge that with each passing day their health is improving and they are undoubtedly fitter and healthier than they have ever been.

A plant based lifestyle for dogs can help eliminate skin and fur complaints, stomach and intestinal problems and hyperactivity, all of which may be caused by the consumption of meat and animal by-products. FACT: Half of all adult dogs will get cancer. Let's face it dogs today aren't as healthy as their ancestors, which is strange because veterinary medicine is more advanced now than ever. But if your dog suffers from chronic diseases like arthritis, skin issues, obesity, ear infections, heart disease, digestive issues, diabetes or cancer, they are not alone...Most dogs do!

In this first edition I have tried to focus on simple dinner and treat recipes that people can introduce into their daily routines without too much fuss. Plus I have chosen ingredients that you should already have in your store cupboard so that the transition will be a simple and cost effective one. I congratulate anyone for having an open mind and to think outside the propaganda box. We all continue to learn throughout our years on this planet and theories do change, new scientific studies into foods are being conducted everyday, but what you must do is research these ideas yourself and then form your own conclusion. This is the only way to experience your own personal awakening on health and nutrition for your canine friend.

VEGANISM AND ANIMAL RIGHTS

Many people may suggest that feeding a dog a vegan or vegetarian lifestyle is against nature and their animal rights; after all dogs have canine teeth? Perhaps I can suggest to you that preventing dogs from hunting their own food, treating them like humans, dressing them up and keeping them prisoners is also in this same category, as well as feeding dogs animals, such as cows or horses etc, purely because a dog could not and would not hunt and kill them for consumption if they were undomesticated. Could you imagine your own dog hunting, bringing down and killing a cow? No neither can I. More to the point is that untamed dogs would never consume the animals most commercial dog food companies use as part of their ingredient list. Most importantly the meat used for commercial pet foods [4D meat] is not fit for human consumption and therefore threatens the health and well-being of our canine companions. I believe that we have a moral responsibility to reduce animal suffering which in turn helps conserve the planet. Nutritional plant based foods [which I will get to later] are economically and widely available in today's modern society and therefore there is no excuse to kill sentient beings to feed our pets.

People believe that dogs are true carnivores because of their teeth and jaw structure, used for pulling down prey, tearing at flesh and grinding down bones. Furthermore people believe that eating flesh is fundamental to dogs' health, be it raw or cooked. I believe that dogs are omnivores. An omnivore is an animal that derives its energy and nutrients from a diet consisting of a variety of food sources. Firstly, it is a well known fact the largest mammal having canine teeth of any land animal belongs to a true herbivore, the hippopotamus. Nearly all mammals have canine teeth but not all eat meat. In fact, several herbivores have ferocious canine teeth, including the gorilla and gelada baboon. My point is that evolution has made animals seek out other foods available and their bodies have changed. After all, look at how your dog eats grass when you are out on walks or in your garden. If you see your dog eating more young fresh sprouting grass this may simply mean he is seeking vegetation to gather the nutritional enzymes needed. Dogs that eat rye type grass may suggest that this is suitable to bind something that does not agree with his system, but there are many theories on this subject that you may wish to research yourself.

I believe that all animals have the right to live and so I choose to feed my dogs a vegan lifestyle. Also the commercial pet food industry is not putting the health and welfare of our companion animals first, by neglecting to tell us what is *exactly* in their food products, but we will come to this subject later in the book.

It is important to point out that most livestock animals live in barbaric conditions known as battery farms. These animals are kept in isolation and destined for death behind closed doors in slaughterhouses, which is not, I am sure, the way you would like to spend or end your life. The lives of factory farmed animals in today's society are not worth living. They are fed and injected with various hormones and chemicals in their short lives and slaughtered behind closed doors in the most appalling and horrific ways. We all have the right to choose which foods we eat and perhaps if humans were educated on this subject at an early age many animals may stand a chance of a life worth living. Statistics show; 2.5 million animals are killed every day; 100,000 an hour; 1700 per minute and 30 every second. This figure doesn't include fish, which are killed in such vast numbers that they are counted in tonnes. I believe all animals are innocent and vulnerable, just like your dog and therefore I cannot see any reason for killing another animal to satisfy appetites when it has been proven scientifically that the goodness in plant based foods are nutritionally superior.

WHY VEGANISM FOR DOGS?

I find it quite interesting how some foods (especially plant based) create such controversy in the canine fraternity, whilst other foods have been part of mainstream canine diets for so long no one seems to challenge them. Generally anything new to us in life we have a hard time trying to come to terms with, simply because we have been conditioned to think otherwise; just like eating meat for example. It is always worth conducting your own research and then discover your own conclusion as to what you believe is right. Not everyone is classed as an expert and just because it is on the internet does not mean that it is fact, but more an overall general opinion. Whilst veganism isn't for everyone I pat anyone on the back for wishing to learn more about living a cruelty free existence. Once armed with all the knowledge and education then it is up to oneself to make the decision one way or the other. However, domesticated dogs do not have the luxury of choices; they are given what their guardian wants to feed them through personal views, opinions and income available. Dogs are also told what they are or not allowed to do and sadly many have strict boundaries. Dogs have no biological need for products such as cows' milk, cheese or dairy products. In fact many dogs are lactose intolerant, they do not produce the enzyme Lactase, and therefore they are unable to break down Lactose (milk sugar). This can cause gas, diarrhoea and abdominal discomfort and because of the higher saturated fat content in dairy products this can increase skin inflammation, digestion problems and faster ageing of the body's cell production. Studies have proved that the excess mucus caused by dairy products can harden to form a coating along the inner wall of the intestines which hinders the absorption of nutrients, whilst raw egg whites contain a protein called Avidin. This protein depletes the dog of B vitamins, specifically Biotin, which is essential to growth and coat condition. Also, raw eggs may contain bacteria, such as Salmonella which often leads to symptoms such as gastroenteritis, fever and shock.

Current research out of the University of Davis, California and the University of Uppsalla in Sweden independently suggests that modern canines have evolved to develop the digestive enzymes to break down starches and plant-based proteins. This process began approximately 7,000 years ago with dogs that migrated to South East Asia and who thrived on a rice-based diet. One survey conducted by PETA (People for the Ethical Treatment of Animals) in 2004 found that 82 percent of dogs that had been vegan for five years or more were in good to excellent health and that the longer a dog remained on a vegetarian or vegan diet, the greater the likelihood that the dog would have overall good to excellent health. This study of 300 vegetarian companion dogs found that in general, vegetarian and vegan dogs are healthier than their non-vegetarian counterparts. The research also found that nutritional yeast and garlic appear to be beneficial to overall health and to coat condition.

Many people feel that feeding a wealth of vegetables to a dog's diet may have the consequence of diarrhoea, I reply quite to the contrary. Fibre is only found in foods that come from plants and are either soluble or insoluble. Both types of fibre are equally important for canine health and digestion, preventing conditions such as diabetes, heart disease and obesity. Soluble fibres are the element of plants that break down in the stomach. Soluble fibre attracts water and forms a gel, which slows down digestion and delays the emptying of the stomach and makes the dog feel full which can help control weight. Insoluble fibres add bulk to the dogs' diet and are considered gut-healthy fibre because they help prevent constipation. These fibres do not dissolve in water; they pass through the gastrointestinal tract relatively intact and speed up the passage of food and waste through the gut. Both of these fibres assist the body in different ways, so a healthy canine diet should include both types to promote regular bowel movements and can only be absorbed from vegetables and grains, never from meat.

Soluble fibre is found naturally in many plant foods that are suitable for dogs, such as oats, apples, bananas, linseeds, root vegetables and carrots.

Insoluble fibre is found naturally in many plant foods that are suitable for dogs, such as whole grains, legumes, corn, nuts, seeds and brown rice.

In my opinion nutrition is the fundamental key of animal care and by having the tools to be able to feed your pet well will aid longevity as well as cutting down the visits to your local veterinarian. Let's not forget Bramble the border collie who lived on a vegan lifestyle until she was 25 years old which earned her consideration by the Guinness Book of World Records as the world's oldest living dog in 2002.

Commercial dog food may have serious behaviour effects, as well as negative impact to general health and well being, because many commercial dog foods contain additives, colourants, and preservatives. Some of these additives can and do affect our dogs health dramatically. As a canine psychologist I notice a dramatic difference to a dog's well being, as well as behaviour, depending on what they are fed. Additives, colourants and preservatives tend to have the effect on dogs much like the equivalent to the label ADHD in children who are given high sugar and processed foods, which leads to hyperactivity and unwanted behaviour as well as lethargy.

A vegan diet can bring relief. I've seen many dogs with food allergies, aggression and mood swings that often by switching to a plant based diet can help them achieve body balance. We've seen a lot of cancer and other degenerative diseases in dogs in recent years so it is easy to suspect that commercial pet food could well be a contributor. The effects of nutrition and behaviour have been studied and ingredients with high levels of Tryptophan and lower levels of Tyrosine, are useful for combating aggressive behaviour. Dogs need a certain amount of energy to sustain the normal activities of their daily lives. Growth, pregnancy, lactation, and exercise all increase these normal energy requirements. Generally measured in terms of calories, energy comes from three major dietary components: carbohydrates, protein, and fats.

Those guardians who have already embraced a vegan lifestyle for their canine companions say they have living and breathing proof that it works.

HEALTH AND NUTRITION FOR VEGAN DOGS

A healthy immune system is essential to maintain good overall health and aid longevity in dogs. The dog's immune system thrives on a vegan lifestyle because the body absorbs the goodness from the nutrients in plant based foods. In my studies I found that omitting processed foods, together with no annual boosters, is the key to good health and longevity in my canine companions. There is a huge body of evidence to prove that yearly booster injections are not just harming and killing our dogs but is once again another way of lining the manufacturer and veterinarians pockets. Instead of over vaccinating your dog ask your veterinarian to conduct a Titer Test to establish whether your dog requires the vaccines instead. By doing so it also gives you, the guardian more control in how you care for your dog plus you may well be helping to educate other people to do the same. I find that more and more dog guardians are moving away from conventional vaccinations completely and opt for homoeopathic nosodes. You can read more about nosodes, over-vaccinating and Titer tests in the reading resources section.

Dogs need several different kinds of nutrients; amino acids from proteins, fatty acids and carbohydrates, vitamins, minerals and fresh water. I believe that food is the medicine to achieve good health and aid longevity. It's quite simple; Mother Nature has provided us with a variety of food sources to make sure we absorb all the relevant nutrients to stay healthy. Humans introduced fake processed food whilst also adding addictive and cheap ingredients just simply because of the financial gain rather than a beneficial product for our dog's health which sadly in today's society is very poor indeed. Whilst we are now starting to see more conscious and ethical pet food companies, these are very few and far between and are relatively small in comparison to the large commercial dog food companies. These work with veterinarians to push you into buying them by ploughing millions of pounds into clever marketing campaigns, making you believe that you are buying the best food for your beloved dog.

Studies have proved that good nutrition is crucial to good overall health and aids longevity in dogs. But did we not know this already? Surely this is obvious? If you ate poorly processed foods for years how do you think your body would feel and look from the inside out? Yes rather tired and poor I would imagine. So why would we not think our dogs feel the same, lethargic, ill and bored of the same bland foods day in day out.

On a more positive note, the UK has started to see more veterinarians advising and guiding dog guardians towards complementary therapies to provide better care on a holistic basis; this also includes incorporating feeding plant based foods. Whilst many of these studies into veganism for dogs are held in high regard in the US, the UK is definitely catching up with studying the health benefits of a fresh home made diet. Studies have also found that dogs fed on a natural varied diet have a better sense of smell, so the overall health of your dog thrives in many ways. So really all the experts are now saying is that if we feed our dogs a more natural lifestyle they may well live even longer than their biological clock determines. Interesting stuff eh!

There is no doubt that dogs thrive on a plant based lifestyle, the proof speaks for itself and contrary to what pet food manufacturers lead you to believe, a variety of foods is the key to good health and longevity. Just think, if you ate the same food day in day out, how would you feel? Not just bored but your body would crave different foods. This is the body's way of telling us that we need different nutrients to be able to function. Many dogs with food allergies have been found to thrive on a plant based diet, because the most common allergens are beef, dairy products, chicken, lamb, fish, eggs, corn, wheat, and soy. The symptoms of food allergies are itchy skin, recurrent ear infections, hair loss, excessive irritation scratching, digestive stress, hot spots, foot chewing, diarrhoea and skin infections. If you find your dog has a food allergy the best course of action is to try and incorporate a home made meal once or twice a week to start with, this way you can determine if the symptoms decrease whilst also seeing how your dog enjoys the flavours, taste and variety. I find that if my dog doesn't like the smell or taste of something that this is his body's way of saying that he does not require it; instinctively they know. Many dogs have allergies and this is where commercial pet food companies brain wash people into believing that their product provides all the nutrients the dog needs in a single meal and also in the correct proportions to be able to reduce allergies. However, they fail to state that balance needs to be achieved over a period of time and not at every single meal, which is extremely important for the body to function naturally.

Our domesticated dogs are very far removed from their ancestors. Our canine friends have evolved to eat a diet very similar to what we eat. Its entire physiological make up has changed over the centuries to metabolise a diet rich in vegetables, quality grains and pulses. Historically our pets have been fed table scraps and stolen titbits and their metabolism has adapted to accommodate the variation. Our dogs can no longer digest copious amounts of raw meat and most dogs actually prefer a diet that is rich in vegetables and nutritious pulses.

So this leads to the next controversial question; are dogs carnivores? Contrary to many human beliefs dogs are in fact omnivores; natural scavengers that will eat anything to survive. Dogs do not produce amylase in their saliva like we do and therefore digestion does not occur until food reaches their stomach. Amylase is the enzyme responsible for breaking down carbohydrates. However, decades of research proves that dogs do digest grains and starch quite well. Dogs produce potent pancreatic amylase as well as enzymes to digest carbohydrates. Canine digestive physiology resembles human digestive physiology, but vegetables should be shredded or blended to derive the nutritional benefits contained in them.

Many guardians choose to add extra digestive enzymes to their dogs food but I will go into that more in the supplement chapter and you can then make the decision for yourself.

Although protein is essential to our canine friends not all proteins function equally, with protein qualities varying enormously between various sources. Three factors affecting protein quality include: protein source, amino acid composition and digestibility. Simply stated, minerals, vitamins, protein and hormones cannot function without enzymes being present. Enzymes in turn, cannot function if the cells are too acidic if exposed to heat, like most processed pet food. Meat is very high in phosphorous which can cause severe lack of calcium, magnesium and other essential minerals. Vegetables and herbs are great sources of magnesium and calcium, particularly seen in green leafy vegetables.

It is no wonder that many of our companion animals are malnourished and suffer from a wide spectrum of illness; from skin conditions to digestive problems, cancer, diabetes, arthritic conditions, renal complications, heart disease, dental disease and epilepsy. So reading all the information and resources available throughout the years, we now know that feeding a complete balanced and highly digestible diet with quality ingredients and filtered water is the key to good health and nutrition.

The debate is ongoing about how much protein is too much for a dog's diet. While I think it is best to provide a variety of foods, I think we need to fixate less on worrying about too much protein and be more concerned about the *quality* of the protein. Ingesting and processing high quality protein does not strain and damage a dog's organs the way poor quality protein does. This is one reason why you need to be mindful of the protein source in the commercial food you feed your dog.

Over the last decade there has been a definite increase towards natural health products for companion animals, simply because of the demand. Because of this demand a large amount of veterinarian clinics are now offering alternative therapies, such as, homeopathy, acupuncture, herbal remedies, healing methods and much more. Working together with these alternative methods is closely linked to how we feed our dogs which is part of the whole change of thinking. This has resulted in people making a stand and saying *no* to unnecessary conventional drugs and *no* to feeding commercial pet foods and moving towards nutritional supplements and natural feeding methods, to help maintain good health. Practising veterinarians are invariably linked to the commercial pet food industry. They advocate and even market a certain brand of commercial food in their surgeries for which they receive substantial revenue and benefits. Whilst training, veterinary students are taught that commercial foods are best for pets. Some may question this and a portion of those that challenge these orthodox teachings tend to be holistic practitioners and go on to support natural feeding. I find this a very positive change in the balance; I can imagine the pet food industry is very nervous indeed and if not, they should be.

People always ask me one fundamental question about feeding my dogs a vegan diet, 'so what about protein?' Many commercial dog foods actually have a very small percentage of protein so by providing nutritional balanced home cooked meals they actually eat more quality protein. I am a firm believer in the fact that if the quality isn't good enough for me, then it is not good enough for my canine friends. Whichever food lifestyle you choose to feed your dog all I can advise is that you conduct your own research and then decide on the best course of action from your conclusion. Dogs deserve longevity and as their guardians we must give them the right levels of nutritional food, exercise, love and stability in their lives so they stay family members for longer, live happy and healthy lives, with fewer visits to the vets. Mother Nature has provided us with an abundance of raw materials; all we need to do is use them.

Essential Amino Acids | High-Content Plant-Based Foods

Dogs require 22 amino acids to handle their metabolic and energy requirements; functions including structural (muscle and fur) as well as physiological (enzymes and chemical messengers). However, the canine body can only produce 12 of the 22. The other 10 must come from the food they consume.

The ten essential amino acids and suggested foods for dogs include:

Arginine = Spinach, soy beans, oats, quinoa, seaweed spirulina, pumpkin and sesame seeds.

Histidine = Kidney beans, rice, sunflower seeds, tofu, cauliflower, bananas, wheat and rye.

Isoleucine = Lentils, soy products, spinach, most seeds, alfalfa seeds, chickpeas and pinto beans.

Leucine = Tempeh, dried spirulina, white and kidney beans, lentils and soy based foods.

Lysine = Black beans, lentils, parsley, peas, watercress, apricots, sunflower seeds and peanuts.

Methionine = Sunflower seeds, oats, sweet corn, edamame (raw), rice, peach, kiwi.

Phenylalanine = Chickpeas, pumpkin, soy products, broad beans, dried fruit and lentils.

Threonine = Edamame (raw), watercress, sunflower seeds, peas, watermelon and split peas.

Tryptophan = Spinach, almonds, pumpkin seeds, beans, lentils, oat bran and pineapple.

Valine = Spaghetti, lentils, most beans, potato, peanuts, broccoli, banana and oranges.

Amino acids are the building blocks of protein. It's the substance protein is actually made of that is considered essential, not the protein itself. The canine body requires amino acids in order to make structural proteins and enzymes that carry out biochemical reactions. The body also uses amino acids to produce hormones, neurotransmitters and other important bio chemicals. The right combination of vegetable proteins can satisfy a dog's amino acid requirements. So don't count proteins, count amino acids!

COMMERCIAL PET FOODS | THE TRUTH

Not all commercial dog foods are bad for dogs, just most of them. Numerous commercial pet food products are deplorably deficient in key nutrients and full of toxic junk and fillers that provide no nutritional benefit for our canine friends. Many people do not enjoy or wish to feed their dogs meat, dairy or eggs and often only do so simply based on the assumption that they have to. Yet others do not realise the negative health, economic and environmental impacts of feeding their dogs these animal waste products.

Luckily many dog guardians have learnt to analyse pet food labels for meat terminology, order of protein and grain sources and the presence of artificial preservatives. But how many people actually know how to review the long list of vitamins and minerals on the label, and more importantly what they all mean? Hopefully there is enough information in this first edition for you to be able to analyse most pet foods.

Most large pet food manufacturers are owned by global conglomerates and market their products in a very clever way, spending hundreds of thousands of pounds on marketing and public relations so that the consumer believes that they are buying a quality premium product fit for their beloved companion. Sadly, the ingredients within the cleverly packaged product do little to match the stylish branding. A lot of meat based commercial dog foods contain hormones, pesticides, antibiotics and many are being recalled every day throughout the world because of various contaminations (see more about this in the resource section).

Large commercial pet food companies have been getting away with blinding us with brightly coloured packaging with super cool branding and marketing strategies, that make us believe that we are spending our hard earned pennies on the best nutritious food for our canine companions. However, the truth about the contents is very different to the packaging and labels lead us to believe. Many popular commercial dog foods use cheap low grade ingredients, not to mention using ground up parts of animals that were not fit for human consumption which fall into the 4D category; Dead, Dying, Diseased and Disabled.

Most animal feeds are made using 4D meat which is animal waste processed in rendering plants. However, this same system which converts waste into animal feed has also evolved into a recycling nightmare. Dead, dying, diseased and disabled animals are accompanied by a host of unwanted contaminants, including pesticides processed via tainted livestock and fish oil which is commonly contaminated with mercury and other heavy metals. Sadly this also includes slaughterhouse waste, culled wildlife, road kill carcases, euthanised cats and dogs from veterinarians and rescue centres (some with their flea collar still attached), restaurant greases and recovered cooking oils, dead zoo animals and many many more shocking so called *ingredients.* Antibiotics and other pharmaceuticals follow livestock directly into the 'hoggers' (the large vats used to grind and filter animal tissues prior to deep-fat-frying) and even the drugs given to euthanise animals have been regularly found in the rendered product.

Sadly, the vast majority of commercial dog food sold in supermarkets use meat and animal derivatives as their main ingredient, which is clearly labelled on their packaging. However, because most products are not manufactured in the UK the term 'meat and animal derivatives' is a very loose word, simply because the laws or customs in other countries are different. The term can be used for very low grade animal products including some that are nutritionally very poor. Also, because the species isn't and doesn't have to be specified, manufacturers are able to change their meat source between batches depending on what is available at the time. Pet foods labelled with 'meat derivatives', 'animal by-product meal', 'meat by-product meal' or 'animal fats' are all products of this shocking rendering process and it is wise to eliminate these products immediately from your dog's diet as they serve no nutritional benefit at all.

As well as meat derivatives (4Dmeat) the dog food content list includes unidentified cereals, sugars, fats, vegetable derivatives, colourants, antioxidants and preservatives. If you look closely the meat content will be the very legal minimum required by legislation. Also E numbers we now know are harmful, especially E numbers such as E172, E320, E321, E110 plus many more which have been banned in various countries because they have been proven to cause severe health complications. If your dog has chronic skin and coat problems, itching, scratching, hair loss and food intolerances it is most likely due to the contents of his food.

If the quality of ingredients in dog food is not fit for human consumption then why would anyone feed it to their dog? It is a well known fact that the use of E numbers in human food have adverse effects on our children. Therefore people must also educate themselves more about dog food. I have heard many people against feeding a natural diet and some even say 'modern society does not have the time to spend preparing nutritionally balanced meals for its pets'. How very sad is that statement! It is a bit like saying 'modern society does not have time to spend preparing nutritionally balanced meals for its children'. So the excuse is just that, no one has the time. So let's all feed our loved ones junk food, for ultimately that is what dog food is, junk food for dogs. Problem is with this feeding ethic, when dogs become ill no one seems to point the finger in the direction of the foods that they have consumed. As dogs age internal organs such as heart and kidneys lose metabolic flexibility. Healthy tissue reserves get less over time and this simply means that organs take longer to process the intake of inferior foods and we then see a decline in health. This is why we see in shops that dog food is directed at age groups, i.e. puppy food, adult, senior etc, they are simply suggesting that essential nutrients should change in their diet as the dog ages. Guardians that choose to feed cheap commercial foods, that use inferior ingredients, are certainly not considering the long term health benefits of their dog. Scientific studies have proven that eating meat can increase chances of cancer. Whilst one never knows what the future holds, eating a plant based lifestyle will significantly reduce the chances of cancer causing illnesses. We now know that many commercial pet foods contain slaughterhouse wastes, toxic products from spoiled foodstuffs, non nutritive fillers, heavy metal contaminants, pesticides, herbicides, drug residues, sugars, artificial colours, flavours, and preservatives. That is why it is so important for all dog guardians to be able to spot these dubious ingredients and avoid buying these products that have been made using these questionable contaminated materials.

It is also worth mentioning the laboratory testing of dog food whilst on the subject. After uncovering extensive abuse of dogs and cats at a testing laboratory for pet food manufacturer iams, PETA contacted hundreds of companion animal food companies to ask if they conduct laboratory tests on animals. None of these tests are necessary or required by law, and humane alternatives do exist. Non invasive, non lethal, and cage free "in-home" testing is conducted by PetSci, and collaborative veterinary clinic studies allow sick animals who are volunteered by their guardians, to participate in humane feeding trials that can determine the beneficial effects of nutrition on a specific illness. In the resources section of this book is a list of companies that have assured PETA in writing that they do not test on animals in laboratories. Companies that are not on this list responded to say that they *do* conduct laboratory experiments on animals or failed to respond to PETA's numerous enquiries and are therefore assumed to conduct laboratory experiments on innocent animals.

This subject is a never ending nightmare with conglomerate companies blinding consumers with clever marketing relations and with more and more pet foods being recalled including lawsuits claiming deaths of thousands of pets, it is a wonder anyone buys commercial pet food at all. There is a wealth of information out there on this subject and if the beforehand hasn't put you off, then do more of your own research and find the truth out for yourself, you will find yourself making wholesome home made food before you know it.

Since I graduated from veterinary school in 1965, I've noticed a general deterioration in pet health. I believe that the chemical additives in pet food play a major part in that decline - **Dr Richard Pitcairn**

THE PROTEIN MYTH | PLANT AND ANIMAL PROTEIN SOURCES

Many people believe that plant based foods do not provide protein or not *enough* protein or are sources of an inferior type of protein. But are these ideas correct? The scientific truth is that plant based foods *do* have the protein that dogs require, and contrary to the popular myth they are indeed a complete protein source. If we are to move forward in the quest for canine health we first have to encompass the correct information. Yet despite living in the age of information with a wealth of knowledge at our fingertips, this is actually quite a challenge. The internet for example is infiltrated with misleading or flawed information being passed around from one article to the next. I suggest that you do your own research and ask the question, where did this information come from? And who is behind the research? It isn't until we actually do enquire that we expose some interesting new revelations. Our mainstream media, whether radio, TV or print does not provide adequate help or research either. It isn't that we all have to agree, because after all there are many view points and contexts from which to consider any situation, but what we must do is clean up some of the mess that has been created, especially by commercial food companies, because it is influencing the health of our dogs in an extremely negative way.

Before we examine the plant versus animal protein myths, let's try to understand the common root behind all of the (mis)information that we have out there today when it comes not just to protein, but the entire field of nutrition. If you have been doing your own personal research, you know that it all points to one area: corporate interests. It is no secret that the meat and dairy farmers are given vast subsidies by governments and unions. Global meat production has quadrupled since the early 1960s from 71 million tonnes to over 290 million tonnes in 2010. On a global basis plants provide 65% of the protein sources and livestock consume a third of the global grain harvest. There is no doubt factory farming has become HUGE business making astronomical profits. It is also a business that can easily proliferate itself if the right ideas are infused into the general populace. Examples of these ideas include fear based conditioning that we all need animal protein for good health, to build muscles or that we need dairy for strong bones. Even though all of these ideas have been exposed today as clever propaganda, they sadly remain heavily ingrained in the minds of the majority of people.

Researcher Michael Bluejay examined and wrote extensively about the protein myth. In his analytical and research based article, 'Setting the Record Straight' he states that this information is neither new, nor a secret. By analysing data from various sources, including the USDA's nutrient database, he shows that plant foods are complete proteins and that they do contain essential amino acids. For example, the largest land animals in the world, elephants, are exclusively vegan. They can weigh up to six tons by eating nothing but plant matter. They certainly wouldn't grow that big if plants were not loaded with protein. Whilst elephants are not dogs it is merely stating a fact that every living creature on the planet requires protein and some of the most powerful land animals are indeed vegan.

The vast majority of the UK population today are making choices based on misleading or incorrect information when it comes to food choices, nutrition and health. When consuming common animal products today people are exposing themselves to numerous health conditions due to the toxicity, pesticides, hormones, drugs and genetically modified organisms that come as part of the package with animal products. So it would be one thing if the animal products were worth it from a health benefit, but today they simply aren't. And given that we now know that plant foods are capable of supplying us with not just enough, or the right type of protein, but even a higher quality protein, whilst protecting our health, it is clear to me which is the smart choice to make if we want to enjoy optimal health and aid longevity, not just for us but also for our dogs, whilst being compassionate human beings.

Plant based foods are practically free from cholesterol, tend to be high in fibre, and are often alkalising to the body. All animal products on the other hand are devoid of fibre, and are acidifying to the body, which causes calcium to be leached from bones, as well as decreasing oxygen levels in the blood and negatively impacting the digestive/lymphatic system.

Scientists now believe it's possible to change the neurological and physical aspects of a dog's brain through nutrition, thus directly affecting their behaviour and intelligence. For example, dogs require both Omega 3 and Omega 6 fatty acids in their diet and both continue to be a major focus of study when it comes to behaviour and nutrition. Omega 3 is found in flaxseed, wheat germ, canola and soybean oils. Major nutrients in a healthy, balanced diet for dogs include protein, fats, carbohydrates, fibre, vitamins and minerals and water. Dogs need to eat a variety of foods to get a good range and balance of vitamins and minerals. Holistic health practitioners firmly believe root vegetables provide important healing properties as well as herbs and spices. They also maintain these vegetables provide stabilising energy that focuses the brain and strengthens the will and therefore has a major effect in how food affects the mood of dogs.

I have never seen a malnourished vegan dog; in fact every vegan dog I have met has been a model of good health and vigour. Whilst all dogs are different in their nutritional requirements, it is up to you the guardian to make sure that their nutritional needs are met and to find the best natural organic sources.

A GUIDE TO GOODNESS IN NATURAL FOOD

Most fruits, vegetables and grains are safe to add to dogs daily meals. Healthy choices like carrots, bananas, peanut butter and oats can be made into tasty treats so good that you can also share. Giving your dog a varied diet is extremely important because they require many different vitamins and minerals for health and vitality, plus it makes meal times more exciting. If dogs were allowed to roam free as nature intended they certainly wouldn't eat the same food every day. Make it fun and be adventurous; your dog will thank you for it! It is really important to point out here that sourcing organic ingredients is most vital; whilst I appreciate it can be an added expense. Before Monsanto, Mother Nature had her own pesticide factory. But sadly most of our produce that is imported will have been tampered with such as Genetically Modified Organisms (GMOs) and other harmful agro-chemicals. GMOs are not adequately monitored to ensure public safety. Long term, independent, peer reviewed studies were not conducted before GMOs were introduced for human or animal consumption. So by purchasing organic products you can be sure they do not contain: fillers, additives, pesticides, by-products, preservatives, artificial colouring or chemical fertilisers. The fact is that organic crops are up to 60% higher in a number of key antioxidants than non-organic crops. Whilst organic produce is slightly more expensive it is well worth paying the extra few pence. With all the concerns over the dangers of GM foods and cancer causing Aflatoxins many people have chosen to grow their own by using a section of their garden or lease an allotment. If you do not have the luxury of a garden you can still achieve a well stocked vegetable patch in very small areas, such as patio pots, window box or balcony, you can even use your window sill to grow herbs. I cannot recommend highly enough to use all organic ingredients for you and your dog. You can read more about organic farming in the reading resources section. So what goodness is in naturally grown food that you can feed your dog?

Fruits are great for hydration and a fantastic source of fibre, potassium, and antioxidants. Apples, blueberries, cantaloupe and blackberries are some of the most nutritious. Discard all pits and seeds as these could result in cyanide poisoning.

Vegetables are pretty much the healthiest foods on the planet. Some of the most nutrition packed are kale, pumpkin, spinach and peas. The varying vibrant colours in vegetables exist because of the thousands of healthful phyto-nutrients.

Nuts and **seeds** are not only a great source of protein and iron; they also support a healthy immune system. Some of the best sources are peanuts, sunflower seeds and pumpkin seeds.

Beans and **lentils** provide a hefty dose of protein and many are also a great source of iron. Kidney beans, pinto beans, lentils and butter beans are some of the best sources.

Grains and starchy vegetables are a great source of fibre, iron, and protein. Brown rice, pasta, oatmeal and sweet potatoes are a few of the healthiest options.

For more information on natural food goodness please refer to the chapter 'Ingredients and their Nutritional Values'.

INGREDIENTS TO AVOID

Before you read the chapter 'ingredients and their nutritional values', I would like to start with food known to be toxic and therefore potentially poisonous to your dog. Knowing what foods to avoid at the beginning is crucial for you to learn to stay away from all those listed below, which are all detrimental to your dog's health. Some of the ingredients, in small amounts, tend to be okay if given occasionally, but some are toxic enough that continuous exposure may cause serious liver damage, anaemia and even death. In my opinion avoid these ingredients at all costs while you whip up treats and snacks for your dog and always check ingredients first to ensure your dog's safety. The following food list is not exhaustive. If you think your pet has been poisoned by one of the below foods you should call a veterinarian immediately. For more information on ingredients to avoid please refer to the resources section.

Apple seeds - Contain cyanide. This toxin inhibits cytochrome oxidase, an enzyme necessary for cellular oxygen transport, preventing appropriate oxygen uptake by cells. When ingested in toxic amounts, clinical signs of dilated pupils, difficulty breathing, inadequate oxygen levels, bright red gums shock and death.

Baking soda, baking powder - Ingested in large quantities and other leavening agents such as dry yeast are poisonous foods for dogs. Typically, these compounds release gases when they react with moisture and heat (in your dog's stomach). This reaction can lead to electrolyte abnormalities (low potassium, low calcium and/or high sodium), muscle spasms and or congestive heart failure.

Caffeine - Most commonly found in coffee, coffee grounds, tea, used tea bags, soda, energy drinks and diet pills. Theobromine, a cousin chemical to caffeine is also found in chocolate.

Chocolate – The chemical toxicity is due to a methylxanthine (like theobromine and caffeine), and results in vomiting, diarrhoea, hyperactivity, inflammation of the pancreas, an abnormal heart rhythm, seizures and rarely even death.

Chives - Part of the *Allium* family, as well as onions and leeks are poisonous to dogs. Clinical signs of anaemia may be seen, and include lethargy, pale gums, an elevated heart rate, an increased respiratory rate, weakness, exercise intolerance and collapse.

Grapes - Grapes, **raisins**, and **currants** are toxic and can result in severe acute kidney failure. These fruits can result in anorexia, vomiting, diarrhoea and potentially severe acute renal failure.

Green tomatoes (especially stems and leaves) - The commonly eaten red tomatoes is considered non toxic but the green parts of the plant contain solanine, though a large amount needs to be ingested for solanine to result in severe poisoning. Ingestion can cause severe gastrointestinal distress (vomiting & diarrhoea), lethargy, weakness and even confusion.

Macadamia nuts - Depending on the amount ingested, clinical signs of severe lethargy, increased body temperature, vomiting, tremors, joint stiffness, and inability to walk (commonly hind limb) may be seen. The toxic mechanism is unknown but can affect nerve function (specifically, the motor neurons, neuromuscular junctions, muscle fibres or neurotransmitters).

Onions - Onion poisoning results in oxidative damage to the red blood cells (making the red blood cells more likely to rupture) and gastroenteritis (e.g., nausea, oral irritation, drooling, abdominal pain, vomiting, and diarrhoea). Onion poisoning may have a delayed onset and clinical signs may not be apparent for several days.

Peach, apricot, plum and cherry pits/stones - The seeds, leaves, and stems of the apricot tree contain cyanide. This toxin inhibits cytochrome oxidase, an enzyme necessary for cellular oxygen transport, preventing appropriate oxygen uptake by cells. When ingested in toxic amounts, clinical signs of dilated pupils, difficulty breathing, inadequate oxygen levels, bright red gums, shock and death can be seen.

Mushrooms – Of all the several thousand species of mushrooms only a small percentage is considered toxic. Clinical signs from mushroom poisoning are dependent on the species of mushroom ingested, the specific toxin within that mushroom, and the individual's own susceptibility. Early clinical signs include vomiting, diarrhoea, abdominal pain, walking drunk, depression, tremors, and seizures, with liver and renal damage occurring later.

Rhubarb leaves - The leaves contain soluble oxalate crystals, with less of the crystals being prevalent in the stalk. Clinical signs of this type of poisoning include drooling, vomiting, diarrhoea, lethargy, weakness, tremors, bloody urine and changes in thirst and urination.

Xylitol - Xylitol is a natural, sugar free sweetener commonly found in many chewing gums, mints, foods (gelatine snacks), oral rinses, toothpastes, and over the counter supplements. Signs of xylitol poisoning in dogs include weakness, lethargy, collapse, vomiting, tremor, seizures, jaundice, black-tarry stools, even coma or death.

MAKING THE ADJUSTMENTS

If your dog has only ever eaten commercial dog food it is important to make the changes gradually over a period of between one to four weeks. The level of detoxification your dog may go through will depend on how healthy they are before starting the process. This is because the body is used to coping with foods such as meat and or by-products which suppress the elimination of toxins. It is normal to expect there will be stages of what is called a natural cleansing process when changing over to a plant based diet. Consuming nutritious foods all in one bowl will discharge the accumulated toxins, so it is therefore important to introduce new foods gradually to allow your dog's digestive system to adjust, whilst also allowing him to get used to the new tastes and textures. If you make the transition too quickly you may see temporary effects such as diarrhoea, passing worms or a loss of appetite which are all quite normal. As the body adjusts to the new transition you may see black stools, which are the cleansing of the colon, as well as strong smelling urine which is the cleansing of the kidneys. You may find that your dog does not accept the new foods well at the beginning but this may be because he is not used to trying different foods, or possibly he just is not that hungry to accept the new transition. The best advice is to persevere, go back a few steps and slowly introduce new foods into his meals until his appetite is able to try new ingredients. Eating a natural diet is a great way to re-energise the body, cleanse organs and tissues, so you may notice your dog has more energy as the nutrients flow through the tissues and increase oxygen in the blood.

Adding new ingredients to mealtimes will depend on your dog's current diet, lifestyle, personality and capability of accepting new experiences. Introducing new foods will be an interesting experience and you will both have lots of fun trying and testing different recipes to see which flavours your dog prefers. Undoubtedly the best time to begin your dog on a plant based diet is when he is a puppy, but adult and senior dogs can convert easily too, however sometimes it may be a longer transition depending on what foods your dog is used to. If your dog is used to a variety of plant foods already then the transition will likely be an easy one. It is well worth speaking to a holistic veterinarian or a canine herbalist first to get a health check to make sure that your dog does not have any underlying health conditions that you are not aware of but also so you can treat any underlying illness and be happy that the change of diet is related to a health condition your dog may already have, rather than the change of his food. It is also important to make sure that your dog is happy and stable before making any radical changes to his diet, such as after holidays, moving home, any new additions to the family, major surgery, bereavement etc.

Too much or too little of any one nutrient can quickly cause upset stomachs so to begin with give a small portion of different foods incorporated into what your dog is used to on a daily basis. You may well find that it is easier to feed textures that your dog is used to in the beginning of the transition. For example, if your dog is only fed kibble, just add a small handful of vegan kibble to his normal version for a few days before slowly adding small portions of home cooked recipes or grated raw fruit and vegetables. You will soon find that your dog will leave the kibble till last and chomp on the fresh plant based ingredients first. Before you know it the transition to a plant based lifestyle will be complete and your dog will soon start to reap the health benefit rewards.

If your dog has a few moderate distresses in the transitional process to plant based foods it may well be helpful to introduce herbs which will help cleanse and heal. You can see more about these in the ingredients list section. When changing over from a commercial dog food, whether you use wet or dry, I find it easier to introduce a vegan branded dog food. I recommend Benevo because their products contain Taurine and L-Carnitine, whilst offering both wet and dry foods. Some are wheat free too so suitable for all dogs' dietary requirements. Benevo is an independent UK based producer of complete vegetarian and vegan pet foods, treats, and accessories, which can be purchased from www.veggiepets.co.uk

FEEDING GUIDELINES

The right food is just as important as feeding the right amount. The actual amount of food your dog requires depends on his activity, age, environment and breed. Always start by following the breed guidelines for your dog's weight; your veterinarian will be able to tell you your dog's ideal weight. The Vegan Dog Nutrition Association recommends that the base of each meal be comprised of soybeans, lentils, rice, oats and various vegetables. At least a third to a half of your dog's meal should consist of a quality protein source. The remaining portion can be made up of a variety of whole grains, raw and cooked vegetables, as well as certain supplemental items tailored to suit your dog's individual requirements. No one knows your dog better than you; I believe that each dog and its food intake are variable depending on age, lifestyle, appetite, metabolism and temperament. So with this in mind I have devised a basic feeding guideline below which is just a guide. It is very important to point out here that dogs should not be exercised within 1 hour before a meal, or 2 to 3 hours after a meal, as this can cause a life threatening condition called gastric torsion or bloat.

What to serve

A basic meal should consist of the following components:

1. Protein: 25-40% of the diet by volume

2. Carbohydrates: 45-55% of the diet by volume

3. Vegetables: 15-25% of the diet by volume

4. Supplements (optional)

For example; if your dog weighs 30lb and consumes around 4 cups of food daily, this equates to 1-1.5 cups of protein, 1.75-2.25 cups of carbohydrate, and 0.6-1 cup of puréed vegetables and or fruits. For protein, carbohydrates, and vegetables, you can select one or more foods from the ingredients list for each meal. Remember, variety is fundamental for your dogs' health and active or working dogs require more percentage of protein to build muscle and repair injuries. Puppies too, need higher protein because they're growing.

How much to serve

I believe that your dog and his appetite will be a good guideline to tell you how much to give him. If you see your dog losing weight then simply give him more until he is at his optimum weight. There is no hard and fast rule, but a dog weighing over 10kg should consume roughly 3% of their body weight in food every day. So a 20 kg dog should be eating roughly 400g. You can serve it in as many meals as you want and at whatever time. For dogs under 11kg, see below.

1kg – 2kg – 10% of bodyweight
3kg – 4kg – 7% of bodyweight
5kg – 8kg – 5% of bodyweight
9kg-10kg – 3% of bodyweight
11kg and over – 2% of bodyweight

It is important to make sure that your dog is eating enough to sustain his energy levels. Some people feed their dogs three times a day but personally I feed my dogs twice a day; so they have breakfast and then late afternoon meal, with various energy boosting treats whilst we are out and about on walks and of course the crucial night time congratulated wee treat!

Bacterial fermentation takes place in the large intestine and transit time through the intestine is 12-30 hours. If a dog is fed much more than needed, the body might respond by rushing the food through in the form of diarrhoea. It is better to feed little and often to find the amount that suits your dogs size and appetite. Obesity in humans is at its highest and we are becoming a nation of fatties, so it is no surprise that we are also starting to see more and more overweight dogs. Dogs that carry extra weight place extra demands on virtually all the organs of their bodies. Therefore, it is very important that your dog is at its optimum weight for his health and is crucial to aid longevity. If you can't see a distinct waistline below your dog's rib cage, it's likely that he is overweight.

I always cook and bake in quantity so I can refrigerate what is left to serve the following day or freeze until required. I always serve my dog's dinners lukewarm or at room temperature not just because my dogs prefer it but it is important to do so because warming the ingredients allows the flavours to waft into the air which your dog will smell with excitement, and don't forget that a dog's smell is his primary special sense. In fact, a dog has more than 220 million olfactory receptors in its nose, while humans have only 5 million, so you can imagine how a warmed up meal would be more appealing! Adjust meals to suit your dog's tastes and needs, we are all different so there are no hard or set rules, make it up as you go along and your best friend will soon tell you if you are hitting his taste buds in the right place.

I have adapted my recipes to try to feed raw and cooked fruits and vegetables so that my dogs get all the nutritional values possible. I would suggest that you start by introducing cooked or steamed vegetables first and then slowly add raw vegetables either grated or pulsed so it is gradual until your dog begs for more! Adding cooked and raw vegetables together is the best way to ensure maximum nutrition but also so that it gives more of an interesting dish that incorporates different textures.

Lastly, water has many essential functions for life, such as transporting nutrients and waste through the body, is required for most metabolic processes, regulates the body temperature whilst lubricates the joints, eyes and the inner ear (for the transmission of sound). Water is a major constituent of the dogs' body so it is essential they have access to clean drinking water at all times.

HOW TO COOK THE BASICS

For storing meals, preserves and ingredients I use kilner glass jars, ziploc and tupperware containers as this is an ideal way to store in an economic, recyclable and environmentally friendly way. Many storage solutions have a vacuum seal which allows the product inside to preserve longer which is a great way to maximise your produce longevity, which as a home baker will prove indispensable. These staple basic recipes will also prove invaluable to you as you venture into the world of plant based recipes for dogs. They will help you gather a larder, fridge & freezer full of food that you can just mix into any other recipe; or if you are short for time then simply add recommended vegan dog brands such as Benevo, V-Dog or Ami, which can be purchased from UK company, Veggie Pets – www.veggiepets.com

Cooking Rice

You can use any rice for this recipe listed in the 'ingredients and their nutritional value' section. Some of my recipes call for cooked rice and others will call for uncooked which is added to the recipe. Cooked rice will keep for 2 days in the fridge in a sealed container and can also be frozen in containers which defrost easily by placing in a sieve and pouring boiling water through to thaw. Some people pre soak rice to remove contaminations; if you wish to pre soak your rice, add to a pan with lots of cold water and leave for 15 minutes before rinsing well.

Method: Pre soak the rice and rinse thoroughly. Add 3 cups of water to 1 cup of rice into a saucepan stir round with a fork and cover with a loose lid. Bring to a near boil and then turn down to a low heat for 10-12 minutes or until the rice has absorbed all the water. Remove from the heat and cover with a tight lid until cooled so the moisture does not escape. Fluff up with a fork and transfer to an airtight container. Rinse rice well before serving to remove the excess starch and toxins

Cooking Beans

Dogs love beans and they are packed full of nutritious protein goodness. If you wish to buy tinned beans then do make sure that they are in water with no added sugar, salt or other unfriendly dog ingredients, plus always make sure you rinse tinned beans thoroughly through a colander before adding to meals or recipes. Buying dried beans is definitely cheaper, especially if you buy in bulk; remember to buy organic if you can. Once open store dried beans in kilner type glass jars that seal completely to keep them fresh, the older beans are the longer they take to cook. I always buy 'Suma Wholefood' products because they are based in the UK and all products are organic. The beans come in large 3kg bags which are very cost effective and store well.

Method: First clean the beans by removing debris or any discoloured beans and rinse thoroughly. To pre soak add the desired amount of beans to a pan and completely cover with filtered water, bring to the boil, cover and leave to stand overnight. When ready to cook rinse the beans thoroughly before adding to a clean pan with a tablespoon of vegetable oil to stop the beans from foaming & boiling over. Cover the beans completely with water and simmer on a gentle heat for the required time. Remember that the beans should always be covered with water in the cooking process and to stir regularly. The cooking process can take anywhere between 1 to 2 hours depending on the size, age and type of bean [always follow the packet instructions]. If the beans are not tender after the specified cooking time keep cooking and repeat the bite test until you get the required tenderness, then drain and rinse immediately to stop the cooking process. Cooked beans will keep for one week in the fridge or frozen for up to three months.

Cooking Grains

There are many types of grains to choose from and the dog friendly ones can be found in the 'Ingredients and their Nutritional Value' section. Grains also serve as flour once milled or flakes which are another great way of adding nutritional value to treats. Grains such as quinoa, millet and buckwheat are great alternatives to brown rice. It is important to rinse grains thoroughly before cooking or adding to recipes. Once cooked millet doubles in weight whilst quinoa and buckwheat trebles in size. Grains take anywhere from 10-20 minutes to cook and always follow the packet instructions; again always try and buy organic.

Flax 'Eggs'

Many vegan baking recipes require an egg replacement which you can purchase from health food shops. However, I find the best vegan egg substitute is to use flax seeds or chia seeds ground up very fine to make meal/powder. When the meal is mixed with water it forms a thick gelatinous consistency which helps to bind other ingredients, but is not suitable for rising purposes. Good health food shops sell flaxseed meal but you can also grind your own flax seed or chia seed meal by whizzing up in a coffee grinder or spice grinder into a very fine powder, then store in an airtight container in the fridge or freezer to keep fresh.

Method: To make one flax 'egg' (multiply ingredients as necessary) Add 1 tbsp of flaxseed meal to a bowl then add 2tbsp of filtered water. Whisk rapidly until the mixture is well combined. Cover and place in the fridge for 15 minutes to allow the mixture to form a gelatinous consistency. Remove from the fridge and stir well before adding to a recipe.

Vegetable Stock

I always make my own vegetable stock for my dogs simply because even store bought stock has many ingredients that are toxic to dogs. Stock is a great ingredient to have in the fridge or freezer to add flavour and moisture to recipes.

Ingredients:
2 carrots, diced
1 parsnip, diced
1 stick of celery, diced
2 kale leaves, chopped
1 clove of garlic, crushed
1 tsp dried parsley
½ tsp dried basil
½ tsp turmeric
½ tsp fresh rosemary, chopped
1 tsp vegan yeast extract with added B12, No salt
6 cups of filtered water

Method:
Add all the ingredients to a large pan covering with water and bring to the boil.
Turn down to a low heat and simmer for 40-45 minutes.
Strain the vegetables from the liquid into a large bowl using a large mesh strainer pressing down to release the excess liquid from the vegetables.
Transfer the liquid back into the pan, place on the lid and leave to cool.
Pour into an airtight container and store in the fridge for up to 3 days.
Discard the vegetables as their nutritional value has depleted.

Tip: Pour into individual portions in an ice cube tray and freeze until required.
Note: Use up any dog friendly veggies that have seen better days.

Gravy for Dogs

Gravy is a great way to add flavour and moisture to meal times, especially for those dogs that love wet food.

Ingredients:
2 cups of vegetable stock, see recipe in section 'How to Cook the Basics'
1 tbsp of coconut flour, sieved

Method:
In a saucepan bring the vegetable stock to a gentle simmer.
Whisk in the coconut flour until completely dissolved and the gravy starts to thicken.
Leave to cool before storing in an airtight container, up to 3 days in the fridge.

Tip: If you require thicker gravy just add more coconut flour until the desired consistency.
Note: Pour into individual portions using an ice cube tray and freeze until required.

Chowder Mix

My dogs love this mix because it smells and tastes doggie divine! You can buy a packet soup broth mix from any health food shop or large supermarket, but if you cannot find a decent mix then simply create your own with this chowder mix recipe.

Ingredients:
½ cup pearl barley
½ cup green split peas
½ cup yellow split peas
½ cup red or brown lentils
½ cup barley flakes
1 tsp vegan yeast extract with added B12, no salt
1 tsp turmeric

Method:
Add the dry chowder mix ingredients to a bowl, pour over cold water just enough to cover, place a lid over the bowl and leave to soak overnight.
Drain and rinse through a mesh sieve then add to a large saucepan.
Pour over 1 litre of warm filtered water, stir in the yeast extract then simmer on a low heat for 20-25 minutes until the chowder mix has softened. Do not let the pan run dry; add more water if required until all the liquid has soaked into the chowder mix.
Stir in the turmeric before placing the lid on the pan and leave to cool before placing in an airtight container, can be kept in the fridge for up to 3 days.

Tip: Always serve tepid to release the wonderful aromas whilst adding more flavour.
Note: Use herbs to add more nutrients and flavour.

Mixed Bean Salad

Whilst it is easy to open a tin, cooking dry beans is cheaper and not as complicated as people think but you can buy mixed bean salads in your local supermarket. Make sure that the bean mix is in water and the contents are organic and rinse thoroughly before use.

Ingredients:
1 cup of chickpeas, cooked
1 cup of red kidney beans, cooked
1 cup of black eyed beans, cooked
1 cup of borlotti beans, cooked
1 cup of haricot beans, cooked
½ cup of vegetable, flaxseed or sunflower oil

Method:
Add all of the ingredients to a food processor and pulse until a coarse consistency.
Transfer to an airtight container and store in the fridge for up to 3 days.

Tip: Fashion into balls, roll in nutritional yeast or crushed seeds for a tasty treat.
Note: Add a tablespoon to various meals to boost fibre and protein intake.

Homemade Seitan Sausages

Seitan is a great source of protein and low in calories. It has a meat like texture so is a great ingredient for dogs that are changing over to a plant based diet. You can have lots of fun with this recipe by using a variation of ingredients. If your dog has gluten intolerance omit this recipe for the vegan sausages instead.

Ingredients:
2 cups of vital wheat gluten
½ cup chick pea flour
½ cup nutritional yeast
¼ tsp oregano
¼ tsp parsley
1 tsp liquid aminos
1 tbsp tomato purée paste
1 clove garlic, crushed
2 tbsp vegetable oil
2 ¼ cups of cold vegetable stock, see recipe in section 'How to Cook the Basics'

Method:
In a large glass bowl mix together the dry ingredients.
In a separate bowl mix together the wet ingredients.
Pour the wet ingredients into the dry ingredients and mix with a fork until well combined; if too dry add a tablespoon of cold water, but make sure the mixture is not too wet.
Cut out 8 individual pieces of tin foil, roughly 30cm/30cm.
Take ½ cup of mixture and place 2 inches in of a piece of tin foil, then form a cylinder sausage shape with your fingers. Tuck in the end piece of the foil over the sausage shape and roll until fully wrapped, twisting the ends to form a cracker.
Repeat the process until you have used all of the sausage mixture.
Add to a steamer for 30 minutes.
Take all of the foil crackers out of the steamer and place on a heat proof surface until cool.
Once cooled unwrap each sausage and cut into slices and store in the fridge overnight allowing the sausages to firm before serving.
Store in an airtight container and keep in the fridge for up to 5 days or freeze up to 3 months.

Tip: Cut into small bite size pieces and use as training treats.
Note: If you want a crunchy outer coating roast off in the oven for 10 minutes.

Vegan Sausages | Soy Free

My dogs absolutely love these sausages. There is no doubt that cooking and freezing your own are the best way to make sure that you know exactly what ingredients go into them, plus you can always omit or add ingredients to suit your dog.

Ingredients:

½ cup yellow bell peppers, finely diced
½ cup of courgettes, finely diced
1 garlic clove, minced
2 tbsp sunflower seeds, pre-soaked
¼ cup sun-dried tomatoes, chopped
1 tbsp liquid aminos
½ cup pinto beans, rinsed
½ tsp fennel seeds, milled
¼ cup brown rice flour
¼ cup nutritional yeast

Method:

Add a teaspoon of oil in a frying pan and sauté the diced peppers, courgettes and garlic for around 5 minutes on a low heat until lightly golden.
Add the cooked mixture to a food processor together with the pre-soaked sunflower seeds, sun-dried tomatoes, liquid aminos, pinto beans and herbs. Pulse to a rough texture.
Transfer the mixture to a large bowl and add the brown rice flour & nutritional yeast.
Knead together well with your hands crushing any lumps.
Take a small handful of dough and roll into sausage shapes then wrap individually in foil.
Add the foiled sausages to a steamer and cook for 30 minutes.
Leave to cool then place in the fridge for 2 hours to help them firm.
If you would like a crunchy crust then bake in the oven for about 10 minutes.
Leave to cool before serving or freeze until required.

Tip: If you want to use bread crumbs to coat your sausage mixture try and bake your own.
Note: Double up the recipe if you have a few mouths to feed or need to store a larger supply. Freeze until required, thaw out to room temperature before serving.

Peanut Butter

I used to buy organic peanut butter for my dog treat recipes but then I noticed that many well known brands started to use palm oil, which is not a vegan ingredient. So I had a go at making it myself and have never looked back! It is the most simple staple ingredient to make and I cannot recommend enough that you try this recipe. I personally add coconut oil to make it creamier, but you can use any oil suitable for dogs.

Ingredients:
2 cups of organic raw peanuts (unsalted)
1 tbsp linseeds
1 ½ tbsp raw coconut oil, liquified

Method:
Add the peanuts and linseeds in a food processor and pulse until ground to a powder consistency.
Add the coconut oil and process for 1 minute on full power and then scrape down the sides.
Process for a further 2 minutes until the mixture resembles a glossy smooth butter.
If you require a crunchy texture then add a few crushed peanuts and pulse a few times to mix into the butter.
Refrigerate for 1-2 hours to allow thickening before using.

Tip: Pre roast the peanuts for 8 minutes for a richer flavour.
Note: If you would like a thinner result use more oil as necessary.

Hummus

Dogs love hummus which is packed full of protein and energy whilst adding flavour and aroma to meal times. Many shop bought variations are not suitable for dogs so it is better to make your own, plus you can add ingredients such as turmeric, basil or dried tomatoes.

Ingredients:
2 cups of chick peas, pre cooked
1 small clove of garlic, minced
1 tbsp of filtered cold water
2 tbsp of tahini paste or 4 tbsp of sesame seeds
2 tbsp sunflower oil

Method:
Add all of the ingredients to a food processor and pulse until a coarse texture.
Scrape down the sides with a spatula.
Process until the texture is silky smooth.
Taste test and add more oil or water for desired consistency.
Transfer to an airtight container and store in the fridge, will keep up to 3-4 days.

Tip: For a low fat option substitute the oil for ¼ cup of silken tofu.
Note: Dogs love raw carrot sticks with home made hummus, a luxury treat!

Apple Purée

I like to use apples that are middle of the taste scale, such as pink lady or empire for apple purée. If I am making dog cakes or treats then I tend to use golden delicious or gala apples as they are the sweetest on the taste scale, whilst bramley, granny smith and braeburn apples are on the tangy side of the scale. You can always mix sweet with tangy depending on what your dog prefers or even add a pear too. Using kilner jars will preserve the purée for longer because they have a vacuum seal. Preserving is both an economic and environmentally friendly way to maximise your fruit and vegetables.

Ingredients:
4 large apples of your choice
½ cup of filtered water
½ tsp ground cinnamon Or ½ tsp fresh or ground ginger

Method:
Peel and core the apples and cut into small chunks.
Add the apples and spices to a small pan with the water and gently simmer with a loose lid until the apples are easily mashed with a fork or potato masher.
Leave to cool and transfer to a glass kilner jar and store in the fridge for up to 7 days.

Tip: Use the apple peel to make crisps, add a very small amount of coconut oil and bake until crisp.
Note: Ginger has been proven to reduce inflammation whilst having anti-cancer effects; according to studies ginger has key benefits relevant to tumours in dogs.

Fruit Compote

With lots of doggie friendly varieties of fruits to choose from it is exciting to experiment with flavours that your dog loves. Choose different fruits from the above fruit section and adapt to suit what organic fruits are in season at your local store or what you have ripe from your garden or allotment.

Ingredients:
2 cups of your chosen fruit
1 tbsp agave nectar
1 tsp lemon juice
3 tbsp chia seeds, milled

Method:
Add all the ingredients to a food processor and blend until puréed.
Transfer to a vacuum sealed preserve jar and refrigerate for 1-2 hours until set into a jelly like consistency.
Store in the fridge until required. Will keep for up to 5 days.

Tip: You can use orange juice if you prefer, just grate the zest and squeeze the juice out of one small orange.
Note: This recipe works great with blackberries and strawberries, even frozen ones!

BREAKFAST RECIPES

I believe that dogs should eat two nutritious meals a day, especially if they are active and most dogs wake up ravenous. My dogs love the variety of breakfasts which consist of oats, a slow releasing energy food to ensure that when out and about on long distance walks their bodies cope with the exercise. Obviously a few wholesome home-made treats along the way are most welcome too!

Porridge

Add 1 cup of porridge oats to 2 ¼ cups of filtered water to a saucepan. Simmer whilst stirring continuously for 4-5 minutes until the oats are soft, and then leave to cool. Add 1 tablespoon of flaxseed meal, mashed fruit or home made fruit purée; stir in well with a little dairy free milk if desired. Make sure that the porridge mixture is tepid or at room temperature before serving with fresh chopped blueberries and strawberries.

Wheat Biscuits with Oat Milk

You can adapt this according to the size and breed of your dog. Add 1 wheat biscuit with ¾ cup of oat milk and mash until very soft; add serving options of your choice.
Stir well, adding more milk if required and serve.
Serving options | quinoa flakes | ground cinnamon | crushed seeds | nutritional yeast | fruit purée | veggie purée | coconut flakes | freshly mashed fruit | tofu yoghurt | flaxseed milled

Brown Rice Breakfast

Add 1 cup of brown rice and 2 cups of filtered water to a pan and stir with a fork. Simmer on a low heat with a loose lid for 10 minutes until the rice has absorbed all of the water. Fluff up the rice with a fork & replace the lid, leave to cool before serving.

Serving options | peas, carrots, fine beans & sweet corn mix | dairy free milk & cinnamon | nutritional yeast | fruit purée | veggie purée | coconut flakes

Polenta Porridge

Ingredients:
3 cups water
1 cup organic polenta
1 cup dairy free milk

Method: In a large saucepan bring the water to the boil. Pour the polenta in a thin stream into the water stirring continuously until the mixture is smooth, and then reduce to a low heat. Cook for 5 to 6 minutes, stirring often. Pour in the dairy free milk and whisk for a further 3-4 minutes, then add any other ingredients and stir until the mixture is combined. (Polenta is cooked when the texture is creamy and the individual grains are tender and the mixture comes away from the side of the pan)
When the polenta has thickened, remove from heat and let stand a few minutes, making sure that the polenta is tepid or at room temperature before serving.
Serving options | fresh fruit | cinnamon | seeds | nutritional yeast | your dogs favourite fruit purée | vegetable purée |

Tofu Yoghurt

Ingredients:
1 ¼ cups organic silken tofu
1 banana
2 tbsp plant based milk
1 tsp apple cider vinegar

Method:
Combine all ingredients in a food processor, blend until smooth and creamy. Add in freshly mashed or puréed fruit such as strawberries and blueberries.
A great ingredient addition to dog treats adding moisture, plus a great filling for KONG® toys which can then be frozen.

Tip: Use any dog friendly plant based milk from the resource section.
Note: Tofu is high in protein, excellent source of amino acids, iron, calcium and other micro-nutrients.

Protein Pancakes

I have based this recipe around the Scottish pancake because they are small and dense. Dogs adore these whilst giving them lots of energy. I add tofu yoghurt and fresh fruit for breakfast or mashed veggies for dinner but you can serve with anything your dog likes.

Ingredients

½ cup quinoa flour, sieved
1 small banana, mashed
2 tbsp dairy free milk
½ tbsp flaxseed, milled
1 tsp coconut oil, for frying

Method

Add all the ingredients to a food processor and blend until thick but smooth batter. Refrigerate for 30 minutes.
On a medium heat melt the coconut oil in a frying pan, then add a round pancake ring (10cm diameter) and ladle in 2 tablespoons of batter. Optional - press a few small pieces of fruit into each pancake if desired.
When bubbles form in the centre and the outside of the pancake, flip over and cook for a further minute until golden.
Remove from the pan and place on a kitchen towel to cool.
Repeat the process until all the batter mixture has gone.
Make sure the pancakes are tepid or at room temperature before serving.
Can be frozen up to 3 months, thaw to room temperature before serving.

Serving options | fresh fruit | cinnamon | seeds | nutritional yeast | your dogs favourite fruit purée | vegetable purée | grated fresh vegetables

Tip: For added fun pour the batter into a large bone shaped cookie cutter.
Note: Organic quinoa flour is one of the most nutritious flours available. Nutrient rich, a source of complete protein providing all of the essential amino acids.

Scrambled Tofu & Vegan Sausages

Scrambled tofu is a great versatile nutritional dish which is quick and easy. A great substitute for those who feed their dogs scrambled eggs, tofu is more nutritious and dogs love the taste. Add nutritional yeast for a nutty flavour.

Ingredients:
1 cup firm tofu, drained and pressed
½ cup bell peppers, thinly diced
1 cup kale, finely chopped
½ tsp garlic powder
½ tsp parsley
¼ tsp turmeric
1 tbsp liquid aminos, optional

Method:
On a chopping board cut the tofu into 1 inch cubes, and then crush with the back of a fork to resemble a crumble texture.
In a large frying pan add a teaspoon of oil and heat. Add the bell peppers, kale, garlic and crumbled tofu and cook on a medium heat for 5 minutes, stirring often so as not to stick to the pan.
Add the rest of the ingredients and reduce to a low heat and cook for a further 5 -7 minutes until the tofu has browned. Stir often to make sure all the ingredients are coated and cooked well, adding more oil if a little dry.
Remove from the heat and leave to cool to room temperature before serving with sliced vegan sausages (see how to cook the basics).

Tip: Serve with the roasted spinach potatoes or toasted wholemeal bread.
Note: Tofu is made from soybeans which are high in protein, calcium and iron.

Quinoa Porridge

All dogs love porridge but using quinoa just adds another dimension. Quinoa is the highest protein grain so very nutritious for dogs. Why not add a few of your dogs favourite fruits mashed or add to pancakes.

Ingredients:
1 cup quinoa, rinsed well
2 cups filtered water
1 tsp ground cinnamon
1 tsp raw coconut oil
½ cup blueberries, or any fruit
Dairy free milk to serve, optional

Method:
Bring 2 cups of filtered water to a simmer in a large saucepan then add the quinoa, cover with a loose lid and reduce the heat and gently simmer for 8-10 minutes until all of the water has been absorbed.
Remove from heat. Add the rest of the ingredients plus a splash of dairy free milk, stir in well and leave to cool.
Serve tepid or at room temperature for best munching results.
Quinoa porridge can be stored for up to 3 days in the fridge.

Tip: For versatility try using mint, anise, peanut butter or agave nectar instead of cinnamon.
Note: Blueberries provide vitamins and minerals including vitamin C, vitamin K and manganese, making them a good choice to help meet nutrient needs.

Pearl Barley & Lentil Dog Meal

Ingredients:
1 cup pearl barley
1 cup red lentils
1 cup yellow lentils
4 cups filtered water
2 carrots, diced
1 cup cabbage
1 cup kale, roughly chopped
½ tsp parsley
½ tsp mint

Method:
Wash the barley and lentils through a wire sieve before adding to a large pan.
Add the filtered water and simmer on a low heat for 15-20 minutes until tender and all the liquid has absorbed (add more liquid if required). Leave to one side with the lid on.
Steam the carrots and cabbage for 10 minutes before adding the kale for a further 5 minutes. Add the vegetables to a food processor and pulse until coarse or mash with a utensil.
Add the vegetables to the lentils and barley and stir well to mix. Leave to cool before serving tepid.
Store in an airtight container in the fridge for up to 3 days.

Tip: Sprinkle sprouting seeds over to serve for an extra nutritional boost.
Note: Kale contains calcium and magnesium which keep bones healthy.

Chickpea Breakfast Bake

Not all dogs can eat soy so this is a great breakfast alternative. If you buy dried chickpeas then simply whizz up a few cups in a grinding mill to make your own flour.

Ingredients:
1 cup plus 2 tbsp of chickpea flour
3 cups plus 2 tbsp of filtered water
½ tsp fresh chopped rosemary
½ tsp ground turmeric
½ tsp garlic, optional

Method:
Preheat the oven to 350 °F | 180 °C | Gas mark 5.
Place a deep baking tray in the oven to warm.
Add the chickpea flour to a bowl. Add 1 cup of filtered water and using a fork or whisk stir well to make a paste. Gradually add more water until the mixture resembles a smooth batter, and then stir in the rosemary & turmeric.
Pour the mixture into the hot baking tray; be cautious because the batter may spit on contact with the temperature.
Bake in the oven for 15 minutes then open the oven door to allow the steam to escape before baking for a further 15 minutes until golden brown around the edges and lightly toasted on the top.
Remove from the oven and run a blunt knife around the edges and score into sections before cooling. To serve cut out squares appropriate for the size of your dog and store in an airtight container in the fridge.

Tip: An oven proof cast iron pancake pan is ideal for this recipe.
Note: A nutritional powerhouse, chickpea flour is high in protein, high in fibre, and iron, plus it's gluten-free.

DINNER RECIPES

I have put together some of my dogs favourite meals so it gives an idea on how to go about incorporating all of the plant based ingredients that are suitable for dogs. Always serve meals at room temperature or tepid, this is because aromas are released and it is more flavoursome for dogs, which is especially important if you are making the change to home made recipes (a simple test is to use the back of your hand or your wrist to see if the temperature is comfortable). Adding herbs and spices is another good way to ensure your dog gets additional nutritional boosts, such as turmeric for example, well known for dogs that may be suffering from the aches and pains associated with arthritis and ageing in general. To boost the B12 content to any dish simply add Engevita nutritional yeast, you will find that your dog will love it!

Vegetable Surprise

The surprise in this dish is in the vegetables that I use, which is basically any that I have on my vegetable rack! You can use any dog friendly veggies that you like, but this recipe is a good start if you are new to plant based vegan cooking for your dog.

Ingredients:
1 cup frozen peas
½ swede, diced
½ cauliflower, cut into small florets
1 large parsnip, diced
1 cup spinach
1 cup chowder mix, see recipe in section 'How to Cook the Basics'
½ tbsp organic raw coconut oil
1 tsp nutritional yeast, to serve

Method:
Add the frozen peas to a bowl that has a lid; pour over boiling water just enough to cover, close the lid and leave to stand.
In a large saucepan simmer the swede, cauliflower and parsnip for 8-10 minutes until al dente. Drain off the liquid and leave the vegetables to one side.
Drain off the peas and mix with the cooked vegetables, add the spinach.
Mash the vegetables together using a potato masher or roughly pulse in a food processor.
Stir in the chowder mix to the mashed vegetables and combine well.
Heat the raw coconut oil until liquefied, and then pour over the vegetable surprise.
Leave to cool and serve according to your dog's daily feed amount with a sprinkle of nutritional yeast.

Tip: If you do not have raw coconut oil then substitute for another oil from the ingredient list.
Note: Nutritional yeast is made from primary inactive yeast, a rich natural source of B vitamins and trace elements.

Bean Bangers

A great recipe that you can freeze and bring out to thaw when time is not on your side. You can add these bean bangers to any other dish such as vegetable surprise to add more nutrition and flavour to whet your dog's appetite. To add variety of nutrients to this recipe use butter beans, pinto beans or kidney beans.

Ingredients:
2 cups cannellini beans, cooked
1 tbsp flaxseed meal
1 tsp liquid aminos
1 tsp tomato purée paste
½ clove garlic, minced
½ tsp parsley
½ tsp basil
2 tbsp coconut oil
1 cup fresh breadcrumbs
1 tbsp nutritional yeast

Method:
Add the beans, flaxseed meal, liquid aminos, tomato paste, garlic and herbs to a food processor and pulse until combined to a coarse mixture.
Turn out onto a board and knead with your hands into banger shapes.
In a separate bowl mix the breadcrumbs and nutritional yeast together and leave to one side.
Melt the coconut oil and pour into a shallow dish to cool slightly to touch.
Dip each banger in the coconut oil until completely covered and then dip into the breadcrumbs until well coated and then place on a lined baking tray.
Grill for 8-10 minutes turning on all sides to achieve a light golden brown crust. Leave to cool before serving at room temperature.

Tip: Shape these bangers into burgers, balls or even bones if you like.
Note: Cannellini beans are rich in protein, high in fibre, low in calories and fat.

Mixed Bean Vegetable Salad

When cooking beans make sure they are washed and cooked until soft. You can buy mixed bean salad in your local supermarket, which will be found in the tinned section. If you do buy in this form for convenience make sure that the mix is in water and the contents are organic and vegan.

Ingredients:
2 cups mixed bean salad, see recipe in section 'How to Cook the Basics'
½ cup green beans, chopped
½ cup sweet corn
1 stick celery, chopped
1 red tomato, diced
1 tsp apple cider vinegar
1 tsp oregano oil
1 tsp fresh parsley
1 tsp fresh mint

Method:
Add all the ingredients to a food processor and pulse until a coarse texture.
Serve tepid or at room temperature with brown rice or pasta.
Store in an airtight container in the fridge for up to 3 days.

Tip: Take a small amount of bean salad and fashion into a ball then roll in nutritional yeast or coconut flakes for a tasty snack.
Note: Add a tablespoon to various meals to boost fibre and protein intake.

Vegetable Pilaf

Pilaf is an old fashioned recipe cooked with rice and a seasoned broth. This is my version of this popular dish for vegan dogs which is a complete meal.

Ingredients:

½ cup brown rice
½ cup quinoa
½ clove garlic, crushed
½ tsp turmeric powder
½ tsp fresh ginger, crushed
1 tsp creamed coconut
1 carrot, diced
1 red tomato, diced
½ cup cauliflower, finely chopped
½ cup yellow bell pepper, diced
2 ½ cups vegetable stock, see recipe in section 'How to Cook the Basics'
½ cup black eyed beans, cooked & mashed
1 cup spinach, roughly chopped
½ cup garden peas

Method:

Soak the rice and quinoa for 10 minutes before thoroughly rinsing in cold water, then leave to drain.
Add 2 tablespoons of any dog friendly oil to a large pan until liquefied.
Add the garlic, turmeric and ginger and sauté on a low heat for a minute before adding the brown rice and quinoa.
Stir the grains and sauté for a further minute.
Add the coconut cream, cauliflower, carrot, tomato and bell pepper, stirring for a further minute.
Add the vegetable stock and stir well before covering with a loose lid, cook on a low heat for 20-25 minutes until the grains are cooked and have absorbed the liquid (if required add more liquid). Remove from the heat.
Add the black eyed beans, spinach and garden peas to a food processor and pulse until coarse then add to the rice and quinoa mixture.
Replace the lid firmly and leave to cool. Serve at room temperature.
Store in an airtight container in the fridge for up to 3 days.

Tip: Broccoli, sweet potato, parsnips, brussel sprouts are ideal alternatives for this dish.
Note: Experiment with various dog friendly herbs, such as alfalfa, aniseed, burdock root or kelp, that way they get the full spectrum of nutrition.

Chickpea Salad

Fresh raw ingredients are fundamental to a vegan lifestyle because it is the best way to ensure all the nutrients and goodness are absorbed by the body. This meal is ideal for dogs on a grain free diet.

Ingredients:
1 cup chick peas, cooked
1 tbsp oregano oil
Salad
1 stick celery, chopped finely
½ apple, peeled, cored & grated
½ pear, peeled, cored & grated
1 carrot, grated
½ cup cucumber, grated
½ cup white cabbage, chopped finely
½ cup kale, chopped finely
½ tsp fresh mint, chopped finely
½ tsp fresh parsley, chopped finely
2 tbsp dog friendly oil of your choice

Method:
Preheat the oven to 375 °F | 190 °C | Gas mark 5.
Add the chick peas to a large food plastic bag with the oregano oil and shake well.
Transfer to a lined baking tray and toast in the oven for 10-15 minutes.
Remove from the oven and let the chick peas cool to room temperature.
Add all the salad ingredients to a food processor and pulse until coarse.
Serve with cooked rice or pasta and sprinkle with crushed sesame seeds, coconut flakes or nutritional yeast.

Tip: Add some sprouting seeds for added bite, flavour and nutrition.
Note: Chickpeas are rich in both soluble and insoluble dietary fibre. Research studies have shown that insoluble fibre not only helps to increase stool bulk and prevent constipation, but also helps prevent digestive disorders.

Quick Cook 'No time to spare' Dinner

Sometimes in life there is no time to stand over a hot stove and cook for hours. This recipe is quick and easy but also allows a complete nutritious dog meal all the same.

Ingredients:
2 cups organic wheat free pasta
4 cups filtered water
1 tsp yeast extract with added B12
3 cups frozen vegetables, ideally a mix of broccoli, carrots, peas and sweet corn
1 tbsp coconut oil
1 cup lentils, cooked
1 tbsp nutritional yeast

Method:
Add the pasta, water and yeast extract to a pan and bring to the boil, then simmer for 8-10 minutes or until the pasta is soft.
Drain the pasta keeping the liquid to one side; leave the pasta to drain.
Add the frozen vegetables to a heat proof bowl and pour in the liquid from the pasta and stir with a fork, place over a tea towel or lid and leave for 5 minutes.
Once the vegetables are nicely tender drain then stir in the vegetables with the pasta.
Gently heat the coconut oil to liquefy then pour over the pasta and vegetables along with the nutritional yeast and lentils.
One good stir and leave to cool, serve at room temperature so all the flavours smell great.

Tip: Omit the pasta for brown or basmati rice and add any leftover veggies.
Note: Lentils help lower cholesterol; manage blood sugar disorders due to their high fibre content which prevents blood sugar levels from rising rapidly after a meal. Lentils also provide important B-vitamins and protein, all with virtually no fat.

Quinoa Protein Power Dinner

Quinoa is a great ingredient to incorporate into a vegan dog's diet because it is packed full of protein. I also like to add a bit of crunch to my dog's meals because they love to masticate and exercise those wonderful jaws.

Ingredients:
1 cup quinoa
1 tsp yeast extract with added B12
1 sweet potato, cooked and mashed
½ cup sugar snap peas roughly chopped
Sprinkle sprouting beans
Sprinkle grated coconut, carrot and apple
Sprinkle ground pumpkin seeds
1 tsp sunflower oil

Method:
Add the quinoa to a mesh sieve and place under running water for a minute, gently shaking to make sure every grain is.
In a large pan add 2 ½ cups of filtered water with the quinoa and bring to a near boil.
Stir in the yeast extract and simmer on a low heat for 15 minutes.
Remove from the heat, cover and stand for a further 5 minutes, then drain and rinse through a mesh sieve.
Add all of the ingredients together in a large bowl and mix until well combined.
Serve at room temperature with raw spinach or roasted pumpkin slices.

Tip: Add a teaspoon of apple cider vinegar to help aid digestion and deter fleas.
Note: Quinoa has a natural bitter coating called saponin, which dissolves when rinsed. It is essential to rinse, wash and cook quinoa before feeding to your dog.

Bubble & Squeak Patties

These are a great way to incorporate left over vegetables. There are no hard and fast rules of what goes into this old fashioned recipe so just use whatever you have to hand, as long as the ingredients are dog friendly.

Ingredients:
1 cup vegetables, cooked
½ cup fresh peas
½ tsp parsley
½ tsp oregano
1 potato, cooked and mashed
1 tbsp tapioca flour
1 tbsp nutritional yeast
1 tsp coconut oil

Method:
Add the vegetables, peas and herbs to a food processor and pulse until a coarse texture then transfer to a large bowl.
Add the mashed potato and mix well, and then shape the mixture into sizeable pattie portions suitable for your dog's size.
In a clean bowl mix together the flour and nutritional yeast and then coat each pattie well, tap off any excess.
Add the coconut oil in a large pan until liquefied.
Add the patties and cook until lightly browned on each side.
Leave to cool and serve tepid with rice or pasta.

Tip: Add a cup of cooked lentils or cooked butter beans for nutritional variation.
Note: For added iron intake use veggies such as spinach and green leafy vegetables.

Macaroni Doggie Cheese

I use this recipe when I don't have much time to spare. My dogs love pasta which is great for when they need carbohydrates for energy on those long walks.

Ingredients:
1 can butter beans, drained and rinsed
1 tbsp soya milk
1 tsp coconut oil, liquified
1 tbsp nutritional yeast
½ tsp turmeric
1 tsp sunflower seeds, milled
2 cups penne pasta, cooked

Method:
In a large bowl mash the butter beans and milk with a utensil or pulse in a food processor.
Add the coconut oil, nutritional yeast, turmeric and sunflower seeds, mixing well.
Stir into the cooked penne pasta until well coated. Store in an airtight container in the fridge for up to 3 days.
Serve slightly warm or at room temperature.

Tip: Use sunflower, hemp or flaxseed oil to add nutritional variations.
Note: Soya milk is made from water and soya beans. Higher in protein than other dairy-free milks, this may help reduce cholesterol.

Buddha Bark Bowl

If you have not heard of a Buddha bowl before then your dog is in for a super nutritious treat! The term Buddha bowl simply means a balanced bowl of tasty healthy nutritional goodness.

Ingredients:
2 cups chick peas, cooked
1 tsp turmeric
½ tsp garlic powder
1 tbsp sunflower oil
½ tsp oregano oil
1 sweet potato, diced
1 tbsp coconut oil
½ cup small broccoli florets
½ cup small cauliflower florets
¼ cup tahini paste
1 cup kale, shredded
½ cup carrots, grated

Method:
Preheat the oven to 375 °F | 190 °C | Gas mark 5.
Add the chick peas to a bag with the turmeric, garlic powder & oils and shake until coated well. Transfer to a baking tray and cook for 10 minutes, remove from the oven and leave to cool.
Add the sweet potato and coconut oil (liquefied) to a baking tray and cook for 10 minutes until lightly brown. Remove from the oven to add the broccoli & cauliflower, stir with a utensil to ensure all vegetables are coated with oil (adding more if not) cook for a further 10 minutes, remove from the oven then leave to cool.
To make the dressing, add the cooled chick pea mixture to a food processor, add the tahini paste and pulse until your desired consistency, if you want a thin texture add 2 tbsp water.
Next crush the sweet potatoes, broccoli & cauliflower with a utensil, making sure to include the oil. To build the Buddha Bark Bowl, start by layering with kale. Then add grated carrot then the sweet potato mix. Top with 2 tbsp of the chickpea dressing, stir if desired then serve.

Tip: This is such a great element of basic healthy cooking for dogs. Stick to the format and you can't go wrong, just vary your ingredients.
Note: The essence of the Buddha bowl is to give the diner a well balanced complete meal, so this is easy to adapt to suit any dog.

Delightful Bow-wow Salad

This recipe is for all those dogs that love fresh ingredients! Use a variation of dog friendly oils to add different sources of nutritional value.

Ingredients:
1 cup organic tempeh
1 tsp tahini
1 tsp hemp oil
1 tsp apple cider vinegar
1 cup brown rice, cooked
½ cup lettuce, shredded
½ cup cucumber, grated
½ cup watermelon, mashed
½ cup carrots, grated
1 red tomato, diced
¼ tsp turmeric, optional
Sprinkle of cress or sprouting beans to garnish

Method:
Whiz the tempeh in a blender until smooth.
Make a salad dressing with tahini, hemp oil, apple cider vinegar and turmeric.
Mix all of the ingredients together in a large bowl until completed coated.
Garnish with cress or sprouting beans and serve.

Tip: You can use mashed sweet potatoes or stir in home made hummus instead of the tempeh to add another dimension to this salad.
Note: Turmeric is a natural anti-inflammatory which helps to reduce the symptoms associated with rheumatoid arthritis and damage to joints affected by arthritis. Turmeric also boosts the liver's ability to metabolise fat and remove waste from the body.

Nutritional Super Dinner

This is a great meal to help boost immunity when dogs are poorly or recovering from an operation. There is a wealth of information out there in regards to immune system boosting herbs. Simply choose the herbs that your dog requires and add in moderation to meals or treats.

Ingredients:

Paste
1 cup kale, chopped
1 cup broccoli, chopped
½ cup yellow bell pepper, diced
1 tsp fresh ginger, crushed
½ tsp garlic, crushed
½ tsp turmeric
½ tsp alfalfa
1 tbsp flaxseed meal
1 tsp sunflower seeds, milled
1 tbsp hemp oil
Additional
2 cups mixed bean salad, see 'How to Cook the Basics'
1 cup lentils, cooked
1 tbsp nutritional yeast

Method:

Add the paste ingredients in a food processor and pulse, scraping down the sides as you go to a thick paste consistency, add more oil if required.
Add the paste to a large bowl. Then add the mixed bean salad and lentils and mix until well combined.
Serve tepid with cooked brown rice or wheat free pasta
Store in an airtight container in the fridge for up to 5 days.

Tip: Add Spirulina or Echinacea for an extra boost to the immune system.
Note: If your dog is fighting cancer or other immune challenges, it is important to feed the right foods to help the body recover.

Raw Dinner Delight

Not all dogs like raw food as a complete meal so if yours is one of them then try and incorporate a few spoonfuls of raw to cooked meals so they absorb all the nutrients as well as getting familiar to different textures and flavours.

Ingredients:
2 carrots
1 courgette
1 small apple, peeled & cored
1 small beetroot
½ cup cabbage, shredded
½ tsp ginger
½ tsp turmeric
1 tbsp nutritional yeast

Method:
Grate the vegetables either by hand or in an electric grater.
Add all the ingredients to a bowl and mix until well combined.
Store in an airtight container in the fridge for up to 2 days.
Serve with cooked legumes, brown rice or wheat free pasta.

Tip: Use a variation of seasonal dog friendly fresh fruit and vegetables for this dish.
Note: Kelp helps strengthen the immune system, reduce arthritic pain, control appetite and aid in weight loss and fight infections. Kelp powder can be sprinkled over any meal.

Canine Sausage Surprise

Show me a dog that doesn't love sausages, once they have tasted this super tasty vegan sausage feast they will be begging for more!

Ingredients:
2 home made vegan sausages see recipe in 'How to Cook the Basics'
½ cup brown rice, cooked
½ cup lentils, cooked
1 cup sweet potato, cooked and mashed
½ cup green beans, chopped
½ cup sugar snap peas, chopped

Method:
Cut the sausages into chunks suitable for your dog's size, leave to one side.
Add the rest of the ingredients to a food processor and pulse until the texture is coarse but blended well, scraping down the sides as you go.
Mix together with the sausages and serve lukewarm or at room temperature.
Store in an airtight container in the fridge or freeze for up to 3 months.

Tip: Use up any dog friendly veggies that are seasonal.
Note: Sweet potatoes are a source of antioxidants which aid healing, whilst fights the effects of ageing. Along with vitamins A, C, B6 and minerals, copper and iron. A good source of dietary fibre which help loose stools.

Millet Mashed Potatoes with Cauliflower

This recipe is not a staple meal but great to add to other recipes to add depth of flavour. Pre make this dish and store in an airtight container in the fridge for up to 2 days or freeze until required.

Ingredients:
1 cup millet, pre soaked and rinsed
1 small clove of garlic, minced
3 cups filtered water
2 cups small cauliflower florets
1 potato, cooked
2 tbsp dairy free milk

Method:
Add the millet, garlic and water to a large saucepan then bring to a boil, place over a lid and reduce the heat to a low simmer for 25 minutes. Do not let the pan run dry, add more water if required.
Add the cauliflower and simmer for a further 5 minutes.
When the millet mixture is soft and thick, take off the heat and leave to stand for 5 minutes.
In a large bowl mash the potato together with the dairy free milk.
Then add the millet mixture and stir through until well combined.
Leave to cool before serving tepid.

Tip: Add nutritional yeast for a nutty flavour and added B12.
Note: Garlic not only adds aroma but aids digestion and supports immune health. Garlic is an antibiotic, antifungal, antiviral, whilst making dogs less desirable to fleas and parasites.

Vegetable Jambalaya

I love making this dish for my dogs; they just adore the different textures and flavours.

Ingredients:
2 tsp hemp oil
½ clove garlic, crushed
1 tsp liquid aminos
1 tsp turmeric
1 stick celery, finely diced
1 red tomato, finely chopped
½ green pepper, finely diced
1 cup brown rice, cooked
1 cup kidney beans, cooked and mashed
2 vegan sausages, sliced see 'How to cook the basics'
Parsley & mint to garnish, optional

Method:
Heat the oil in a pan over a low heat.
Add the garlic, liquid aminos, turmeric, celery, tomato and green pepper; stirring whilst cooking for 2 minutes.
Stir in the cooked brown rice and stir for a further minute to incorporate all of the ingredients.
Add the beans and sliced sausages and stir for a further minute to warm through.
Set aside to cool before serving tepid with a garnish of fresh parsley & mint.

Tip: Use variations of dog friendly rice options, as well as butter beans or black eyed beans to add nutritional variety.
Note: Essential fatty acids are an extremely important part of your dog's diet; hemp oil contains all the essential amino acids and essential fatty acids.

Roast Doggy Dinner

We all know that dogs love the left overs from a Sunday roast, mine simply cannot wait for me to dish up theirs! Whilst dogs adore roast potatoes and gravy it isn't an every day staple to their diet, but we all love a bit of comfort food so why not indulge your dog too.

Ingredients:
1 potato, cut into 1cm cubes
1 sweet potato, cut into 1cm cubes
1 parsnip, cut into 1 cm cubes
½ cup swede, cooked
½ cup broccoli, cooked
½ cup runner beans, cooked
½ cup peas, room temperature
2 tbsp vegan gravy, see 'How to cook the basics'

Method:
Preheat the oven to 350 °F | 180 °C | Gas mark 5.
Place the potatoes and parsnips on a baking tray with a tablespoon or two of vegetable oil, give it a shake and cook in the oven for 15-20 minutes.
Add all of the ingredients into a large bowl and mash with a potato masher or pulse in a food processor until coarsely mixed but still a few chunks.
Serve with vegan gravy tepid or at room temperature.

Tip: Store in an airtight container for up to 3 days in the fridge.
Note: Broccoli is a well known super food. Green beans are a great source of dietary fibre, vitamins and minerals. Peas are an excellent source of soluble protein and phytonutrients.

Lovely Mush

This is one of my favourite recipes and from the excitement from my gang when I am dishing up they also think so too! Add a few slices of vegan sausage for even more aroma and flavour.

Ingredients:
½ swede, diced
1 sweet potato, diced
2 carrots, diced
1 cup butter beans, cooked
1 cup black eyed beans, cooked
½ cup peas, defrosted
1 cup basmati rice, cooked
¼ tsp oregano
¼ tsp parsley
¼ tsp mint
2 tsp coconut oil
1 tsp apple cider vinegar

Method:
Steam the swede, sweet potato and carrots until slightly soft, drain and mash.
Add the beans to a food processor and pulse a few times leaving some small chunks to add more bite.
Add the bean mixture together with the mashed vegetables and leave to one side.
Heat the coconut oil in a pan to liquefy and then add to the mixture.
Mix in the remaining ingredients and stir until well combined.
Serve tepid or at room temperature.

Tip: Pre cook rice and store in the fridge see recipe in section 'How to Cook the Basics'
Note: Oregano oil can help treat viral and bacterial infections in dogs.

Lentil & Spinach Burgers

These burgers are ideal for making in large batches to freeze. Take out the night before and thaw ready to add to any meal.

Ingredients:

1 cup brown lentils, rinsed thoroughly
2 cups vegetable stock, see 'How to cook the basics'
2 cups fresh spinach, chopped
1 sweet potato, cooked and mashed
1 cup fresh breadcrumbs
1 tbsp nutritional yeast
½ cup mixed seeds, milled

Method:

Add the lentils and stock to a pan and simmer for 30 minutes until the lentils are fully softened and the liquid is absorbed.
Transfer to a food processor & add the spinach and pulse then leave to one side.
Add all of the ingredients together in a large bowl and mix thoroughly. Cover and refrigerate for at least 1 hour or overnight.
Preheat the oven to 350 °F | 180 °C | Gas mark 5.
Shape the mixture into patties and place on a lined baking tray and cook for 10 minutes before turning over to cook for a further 5 minutes or until lightly golden brown.
Leave to cool before storing in an airtight container and freeze for up to 3 months.

Tip: When shaping the patties oil your hands so the mixture does not stick.
Note: Mill ½ cup each of sunflower seeds, pumpkin seeds, chia seeds and linseeds. Store in an airtight container and sprinkle on any meal to add vital immune boosting nutrients whilst fighting intestinal parasites.

Parsnip and Cabbage Hash

One of the best reasons to make this recipe is for using up any leftovers. Vary the recipe using different beans, herbs and spices. When cooking rice rinse well before and after to remove toxins. Liquid aminos is derived from healthy soybeans that contain 16 essential and non-essential amino acids in naturally occurring amounts.

Ingredients:
1 sweet potato, diced
1 parsnip, diced
1 cup savoy cabbage, shredded
1 carrot, diced
½ tsp garlic, minced
½ tsp ginger, minced
½ cup vegetable stock, see 'How to cook the basics'
1 tsp liquid aminos
½ cup peas
1 cup kidney beans, cooked

Method:
Add the potato, parsnips, cabbage, carrots, garlic and ginger to a large frying pan with 2 tsp of oil and sauté for 5 minutes until lightly browned.
Add the stock and liquid aminos and cook over a medium heat until the vegetables are just tender, about 5-8 minutes.
Remove from the heat and transfer to a large bowl to add the peas and kidney beans.
Mash with a utensil or pulse a few times in a food processor.
Transfer back to the frying pan and tip in the parsnip and cabbage hash, pressing down to make a giant pattie, adding a little more oil if required.
Cut the pattie into small bite size portions and set aside to cool.
Serve tepid or at room temperature with rice or pasta.

Tip: Brush coconut oil on top and flash under a hot grill until golden and the edges are crispy.
Note: Ginger helps boost healthy blood circulation, is a good digestive aid for stomach upsets and nausea whilst helping to keep your dog's teeth clean.

Brown Rice with Chick Peas, Kale, Carrots & Celery

This is a complete meal which provides all the required nutrients, vitamins and minerals.

Ingredients:
1 cup brown rice
1 cup chick peas, cooked
1 cup kale, shredded
2 carrots, diced
1 celery stick, diced
2 tbsp coconut oil

Method:
Add the brown rice to a pan with 1 cup of filtered water and simmer on a low heat until all the water has absorbed, do not let run dry.
Add the carrots and celery to a pan of water and simmer for 8 minutes then add the kale for a further 2 minutes and then drain.
In a food processor pulse the chick peas until coarse then add to a large bowl and keep to one side.
Add the vegetables with the coconut oil to the food processor and pulse then add to the chick pea mixture.
Stir in the cooked brown rice and mix until all the ingredients are well combined and serve tepid.
Store in an airtight container in the fridge for up to 3 days.

Tip:Store in the freezer for up to 3 months.
Note: Fibre in chickpeas can help support digestive tract function.

Spaghetti Bolognese for Dogs

The best thing about this recipe is that we can all share it! Spaghetti Bolognese for Dogs is a complete meal which provides all the required nutrients, vitamins and minerals. Store in the fridge for up to 4 days or freeze for up to 3 months.

Ingredients:
1 clove garlic, minced
1 stick celery, diced
½ cup red lentils, rinsed well
2 carrots, diced
1 tsp turmeric
1 cup tinned chopped tomatoes
½ cup kidney beans, cooked/rinsed
½ cup black eyed beans, cooked/rinsed
2 cups vegetable stock, see 'How to Cook the Basics'
1 tbsp tomato purée
1 tsp liquid aminos
200g organic spaghetti

Method:
Add 1 tsp of vegetable oil to a pan and sauté the garlic and celery on a low heat for 1 minute. Add the lentils, carrots and turmeric and stir for a further minute. Add the tinned tomatoes, beans, stock, tomato purée and liquid aminos then leave to simmer on a low heat for 25-30 minutes, stirring occasionally adding water if required; do not let the pan run dry.
Remove from the heat and stand with lid to cool.
Bring a large pan of water to the boil then add the spaghetti, cook as per the packet instructions. Drain through a colander and run warm water through for a few seconds and shake well. Add to a pan with 2 tbsp of vegetable oil and stir through.
Add a portion of the spaghetti to a portion of the bolognese and serve tepid.

Tip: Sprinkle with toasted wholesome breadcrumbs for extra crunch or sprinkle with nutritional yeast.
Note: Celery is a good source of riboflavin and vitamin B6, whilst having anti-inflammatory health benefits. It is also said to decrease nervousness in dogs.

Grain-free Goodness

A great recipe for dogs that have stomach sensitivities and also ideal for fussy eaters. I am yet to find a dog that cannot eat this dish due to any food intolerance or health reasons.

Ingredients:
2 sweet potatoes, peeled and diced
2 carrots, diced
2 cups lentils, cooked
1 cup chick peas, cooked
1 cup peas
1 large tomato, diced
1 tbsp sun dried tomato paste
½ tbsp sunflower oil
½ tbsp linseed oil
¼ tsp parsley
¼ tsp marjoram
¼ tsp kelp, seaweed powder
1 tsp apple cider vinegar

Method:
Add the potatoes and carrots to a pan of water and boil until tender, drain then mash and leave to one side.
Add the cooked lentils and chick peas to a food processor and pulse to a coarse texture.
Add the rest of the ingredients and blend until puréed.
Transfer to a bowl then add the potatoes and carrot mash mixing together well.
Refrigerate in an airtight container until ready to serve which should be tepid.

Tip: Freeze in individual portions until required, for up to 3 months.
Note: Apple cider vinegar is a natural antiseptic, controls bacteria and fungus growth, improves the dog's skin and coat whilst also repelling fleas and ticks.

DOG TREAT RECIPES

Treats and goodies are always less expensive to make yourself and not as time consuming as people think. Adapt recipes to suit your dog's food likes and dislikes as well as allergies; such as substituting for wheat-free or gluten-free flour which are readily available from health food shops and most supermarkets. You can substitute any type of flour to use in my recipes because it allows you the freedom to use and experiment with different types of flour or what you already have in the cupboard. Don't forget to refer to the ingredients list for flours that are suitable for dogs. Many dog treat recipes out there tend to have eggs in; the best alternative is to use Flax "eggs" which is an easy healthy vegan substitute.

The storage of dog treats is vital to make sure they maintain the consistency that you have created. First rule is that you must make sure that the treats have cooled completely on a wire wrack. I find the best storage solution is a brown paper bag and store in a dry cupboard, this way they keep for much longer, especially the crunchy treats. If you have fresh ingredients that need to be stored in the fridge then simply add the cooled treats to an air tight storage container. If you have made a large batch of treats and wish to freeze them for a later date, just be sure that you have allowed them to cool completely before transferring to an airtight container and treats should keep for up to 3 months in the freezer. It is also quite safe to give dogs frozen treats as long as their teeth are strong and healthy to sustain the crunch!

While you may not have the time or finances to whip up gourmet meals for your dog, one way that you can show him or her a little extra love is by preparing easy, home made vegan dog treats. All you need is a little know-how about canine health and a few minutes of prep time. If you don't have time then instant treats are just as easy, such as carrots, celery, cucumber sticks and banana. I personally love using chickpeas as training treats. Here are a few easy recipes to get you started on the road to a healthy nutritious vegan lifestyle for your dog. Why not impress your friends by baking delicious home made treats as gifts for their dog, put them in a posh bag with a ribbon, ta da!

Carrot & Peanut Butter Treats

These are my dog's favourite treats and we don't leave home without them! They are full of goodness and a fabulous way to introduce new ingredients into your dog's lifestyle.

Ingredients:
2 tbsp peanut butter, see 'How to Cook the Basics'
½ cup hot filtered water
2 large carrots, diced
2 cups organic rye flour
1 cup oats
1 tbsp pumpkin seeds, milled

Method:
Preheat the oven to 375 °F | 190 °C | Gas mark 5.
Mix the peanut butter with ½ cup of hot filtered water from the kettle and mix well into a smooth paste.
Add to a food processor with the carrots and pulse until well combined.
In a large bowl mix the flour, oats and seeds until combined and then add the wet mixture. Mix well to form dough and turn out onto a flour work surface.
Roll out the dough 1cm thick and cut out shapes using your favourite cookie cutter or use a pizza cutter.
Place the shapes onto a lined baking tray and bake for 10-15 minutes until slightly browned.
Leave to cool completely before storing in a paper bag or airtight container for up to 5 days.

Tip: Try not to handle the dough too much, flour or oil your hands before and during the rolling out process.
Note: Use parsnips or sweet potato instead of carrots; it's a really good way of introducing new tastes to your dog's lifestyle so have a play with dog friendly ingredients.

Crunchy Sweetie Treats

These treats are much the same as the carrot and peanut butter recipe but a few ingredients change them into something lovely and sweet and a good way of introducing fruit into your dog's lifestyle.

Ingredients:

1 tbsp peanut butter, see 'How to Cook the Basics'
½ cup hot filtered water
1 small banana, mashed
1 tbsp apple purée, see 'How to Cook the Basics'
1 ½ cups organic rye flour
1 ½ cups oats
1 tbsp chia seeds, milled

Method:

Preheat the oven to 375 °F | 190 °C | Gas mark 5.
In a large bowl mix the peanut butter with ½ cup of hot filtered water and mix well to form a smooth paste.
Add the banana and apple purée and mix until well combined.
In a large bowl mix the flour, oats and seeds until combined and then add the wet mixture. Mix well to form dough and turn out onto a flour work surface.
Roll out the dough 1cm thick and cut out shapes using your favourite cookie cutter or use a pizza cutter.
Place the shapes onto a lined baking tray and bake for 10-15 minutes until slightly browned.
Transfer to a cooling rack and leave until completely cool before storing in a paper bag or an air tight container for up to 5 days.

Tip: Treats store well in the freezer for up to 3 months.
Note: Try using different soft fruits to add a variety of nutrients.

Quick & Cheap Dog Treats

With just two ingredients this is a great recipe for those who do not have a huge larder of ingredients or the finances to match. Oats are naturally gluten free and you can even make your own flour at a fraction of the cost, plus using up any fruit or vegetables you have left over.

Ingredients:
2 cups oat flour
1 cup of puréed fruit or puréed vegetables

Method:
Preheat the oven to 375 °F | 190 °C | Gas mark 5.
Mix the ingredients together to make firm dough (add extra flour or water if required).
Roll out on a floured surface to about 1cm thick.
Cut out as many treats using a round cookie cutter and place on a lined baking sheet, then apply pressure with a fork on each treat before baking for 10 minutes until slightly browned.
So they do not go soft leave the treats to completely cool before storing in a paper bag or an air tight container for up to 5 days.

Tip: Instead of dusting flour on your work surface to roll out the treats why not use polenta instead; this will add a lovely crunch.
Note: Make your own oat flour by processing oats in a food mill until finely ground.

Coconut & Pineapple Cookies

Dogs love coconut and this recipe is a great way to incorporate more flavours into your dog's lifestyle. Make a large batch and freeze in air tight bags or container for up to 3 months. Also good to give as presents to sceptical friends that think dogs dislike plant based ingredients; prepare to be amazed with the canine feedback!

Ingredients:
1 cup pineapple, fresh, diced
1 tbsp flaxseed oil
1 cup coconut, shredded
2 cups organic rye flour

Method:
Preheat the oven to 375 °F | 190 °C | Gas mark 5.
Add the pineapple and oil to a food processor and blend until puréed then transfer to a bowl. Add the dry ingredients to the pineapple purée and mix well to form dough.
Wrap in cling-film and leave for half an hour in the fridge.
Turn out the dough onto a lightly floured surface and roll out to your desired thickness then cut out rounds with a cookie cutter, then place on a lined baking tray.
Prod each cookie with a fork & cook in the oven for 15 minutes or until golden brown.
Leave to cool completely before storing in a paper bag or airtight container for up to 5 days.

Tip: Roll out the cookie dough on parchment paper instead of flour, good tip for rolling out any sticky dough.
Note: Rye flour is easily digested whilst also lowering insulin response and improves blood glucose profile.

Polenta Sticks

Polenta (corn meal) is a great ingredient to use in biscuits and cakes to add moisture and density along with a pleasant grainy texture. Play around with different dog friendly ingredients that your dog loves to add a variety of nutrients to their diet.

Ingredients:
5 cups water or vegetable stock
1 cup organic polenta
2 tsp herbs
1 tbsp nutritional yeast, optional

Method: In a large saucepan bring the liquid to a rolling boil. Pour the polenta in a thin stream into the boiling water stirring continuously until the mixture is smooth and then reduce the heat. Cook over low heat for 6 to 8 minutes, stirring regularly.
Remove from the heat and stir in your chosen herbs and nutritional yeast if using and mix well.
Pour out the polenta mixture onto a cold baking tray and spread evenly about 2 inches thick and leave to cool.
Once completely cool cut the firm polenta into square slices or rounds with a cutter. Brush each polenta piece with a little oil and grill on each side for 2-3 minutes or until golden brown. Leave to cool completely before storing in an airtight container for up to 3 days.

Tip: Use a bone or dog cookie cutter to make this treat an ideal gift for friends.
Note: I use parsley and rosemary herbs in my polenta but feel free to use what you have from the herb section.

Raw Energy Bites

This recipe is great for taking out on long walks to make sure everyone has lots of energy. I like to adapt the recipe to suit what dried fruits I have in my larder.

Ingredients:
½ cup of sunflower seeds
½ cup of pumpkin seeds
1 cup of dried dates, pitted and pre soaked for 1 hour
1 cup of shredded coconut
1 tbsp lemon juice

Method:
Add the sunflower seeds and pumpkin seeds to a food processor and run for 2 minutes until the seeds are milled.
Chop the dates until they are finely diced.
Add the dates and all remaining ingredients to the seeds and blend until well combined.
Turn out the mixture into a lined square tin and press down firmly with your fingers until compact.
Cover & leave to set in the fridge for at least 2 hours before cutting into small bite size pieces.
Transfer to a sealed container and keep in the fridge for up to 3 days.

Tip: Modify the ingredients to suit your dog's favourite fruit.
Note: These no-bake energy bites are gluten-free and grain-free.

Peanut Pillow Bites

These treats are super quick to make and inexpensive too. If you do not want to use peanut butter you can substitute this for lots of other dog friendly ingredients such as mashed pumpkin, banana and apple puree, which are just as delicious.

Ingredients:
1 tbsp peanut butter, see recipe in 'How to cook the basics'
1 tbsp nutritional yeast
½ cup filtered water
1 ½ cups organic rye flour
1 tsp milled chia seeds (optional)

Method:
Preheat the oven to 375 °F | 190 °C | Gas mark 5.
Add all of the ingredients to a food processor in the order above and run to form a dough ball that is smooth and elastic.
Take a small amount of the dough and roll into a ball.
On a clean surface start to form the ball into a cylinder shape by placing your fingers at the centre and gently roll backwards and forwards in an outward motion to make a long snake like shape until your desired thickness, then slice ½ inch pillows with a pizza roller cutter or sharp knife.
Repeat the process until you have used all of the dough.
Place each pillow piece on a lined baking sheet and bake for 20 minutes until lightly browned.
Leave to cool completely before storing in a paper bag or airtight container for up to 5 days.

Tip: If you like your treats extra crunchy just turn off the heat and leave in the oven to cool completely before storing in a paper bag.
Note: Along with a range of other important vitamins, minerals and antioxidants, Chia is the highest plant based source of Omega 3, dietary fibre and protein.

Carrot Muffins

These muffins make fabulous dog gifts which really impress friends; bake in fancy paw printed muffin cases and wrap with ribbons for that added wow factor. I also use this recipe for birthday cakes, simply add all of the mixture to a spring form cake tin and bake, then ice the whole cake with mashed potato and decorate with peas.

Ingredients:

1 ½ flax eggs, see recipe in section 'How to Cook the Basics'
1 small banana, mashed
½ cup apple purée
¼ cup oil, of your choice
¼ cup dairy free milk
1 cup carrots, grated
½ tsp ground cinnamon
1 cup organic rolled oats
2 cups wholemeal flour
¼ cup seeds, for topping (optional)

Method:

Preheat the oven to 375 °F | 190 °C | Gas mark 5.
Prepare the flax eggs and leave to set in the fridge.
Add the flax eggs, banana, apple purée and oil to a bowl and whisk together.
Add the milk and stir, then add the grated carrots and stir again.
In a separate bowl mix the dry ingredients together.
Fold the dry ingredients into the wet mixture until well combined.
Divide the mixture into a greased muffin tray or paper muffin cases, filling to the top. Sprinkle over the seeds (optional).
Bake in the oven for 25-30 minutes or until golden brown. Use a toothpick inserted into the centre, if it comes out clean they are cooked.
Leave to cool completely before storing in a paper bag or airtight container for up to 3 days.

Tip: For an alternative topping press in small pieces of fresh fruit instead of using seeds.
Note: Cinnamon is an anti-inflammatory, great for senior dogs struggling with arthritis.

Apple & Ginger Balls

I love making these special treats for dog friends, they are really easy, plus only take about half an hour! Don't forget that apple seeds are toxic to dogs so make sure they are all removed before adding to the recipe. My dogs love to eat these straight from the freezer plus it's a good method of teeth cleaning.

Ingredients:
2 apples, peeled, cored & diced
1cm x 1cm cube of fresh ginger, roughly chopped
1 tsp vegetable oil
1 tbsp flaxseed meal
1 cup of organic rye flour

Method:
Preheat the oven to 375 °F | 190 °C | Gas mark 5.
Add the apples, ginger and oil to a blender and pulse until puréed, then transfer to a large bowl.
Add the flaxseed meal and flour mixing until well combined. If a little moist add more flour.
Roll the mixture into individual balls, size to suit your dog's bite size and appetite.
Place the balls on a lined baking tray and bake for; 15 minutes if you want a chewy texture or 20-25 minutes if you are aiming for a crispy bake.
Leave to cool completely before storing in a paper bag or airtight container for up to 5 days in the fridge or up to 3 months in the freezer.

Tip: Use the toothpick test to see if the middle of each ball is baked in the centre.
Note: Roll the balls in crushed seeds before baking for added crunch.

Big Banana Bones

These treats are based using a large bone shape cutter, they are hard and crunchy so ideal for a special treat. To give as a gift tie a thick ribbon in a bow around 5 or 6 bones then wrap in cellophane for presentation and protection.

Ingredients:
1 large banana, sliced
1 tsp chia seeds, milled
1 tsp blackstrap molasses
2 tbsp dairy free milk
2 tsp crushed carob drops
1 cup oats
1 ¼ cups chickpea flour

Method:
To a food processor add the banana, chia seeds, black strap molasses, milk & crushed carob.
Blend until smooth, scraping down the sides as you go.
Transfer the mixture to a large bowl, then add the oats and chickpea flour and mix to form a firm dough (use your hands to knead if easier).
Roll out the dough to ½ inch thick. Using a large bone shape cutter, make as many bones as you can, then place on a lined baking tray and bake for 15-20 minutes, until lightly brown.
Remove from oven and place the bones on a wire wrack until cool. Store in a paper bag for up to 5 days or freeze for up to 3 months.

Tip: Treats have to cool completely before storing to keep their consistency.
Note: Research found that fresh banana protects the stomach from wounds, plus bananas are full of potassium and B6. Banana mixed with brown rice is ideal if your dog has a stomach upset.

Sweet Potato Cookies

Rice flour is great for dogs that have allergies or are just that little bit sensitive. These are super sweet for dogs so only give on special occasions, another great present to make for dog friends.

Ingredients:
1 cup brown rice flour
1 cup rolled oats
1 tsp cinnamon
½ cup apple purée, see recipe in section 'How to Cook the Basics'
½ cup cooked and mashed sweet potato
½ banana, mashed

Method:
Preheat the oven to 375 °F | 190 °C | Gas mark 5.
Mix together the rice flour, rolled oats and cinnamon in a large bowl.
In another bowl combine the apple purée, sweet potato and banana.
Make a well in the large bowl and pour in the wet mixture and mix thoroughly until well combined.
Take a teaspoon sized amount of mixture and place on a lined baking sheet.
Bake for 10-15 minutes, or until golden brown.
Leave to cool completely before storing in a paper bag or airtight container.

Tip: If your dog has wheat allergies use buckwheat flour instead.
Note: When purchasing rice flour make sure that the product is labelled as gluten free.

Sweet Potato Chew Strips

I am yet to come across a dog that does not adore these simple treats. Sweet potatoes are nature's supreme source of beta-carotene and a great source of vitamin A. These yummy treats can be baked to achieve a chewy or crunchy texture; test after each hour to see if they have the desired texture you are after.

Ingredients:
2-3 large sweet potatoes

Method:
Preheat the oven to 275 °F | 140 °C | Gas mark 1
Wash and scrub the sweet potatoes.
Cut the sweet potatoes into ½ inch thick strips and place on a parchment lined baking tray.
Bake in the oven for 1 ½ hours and then turn over and bake for a further 1 ½ hours.
Remove from the oven and allow to cool on a wire rack.
Leave to cool completely before storing in a paper bag or airtight container.

Tip: To save on energy, bake when using the oven when cooking other dishes.
Note: You can use a dehydrator if you have one. Set to 125° for 7-8 hours.

Apple & Cinnamon Baked Crisps

These apple crisps are a lovely way to introduce apples for dogs that have not experienced fruit. They are crunchy if cooked on a high setting for less time or chewy if cooked on a lower setting for longer. The apples will reduce in size whilst baking so if you wish to have thick crisps make sure you cut them with this in mind.

Ingredients:
3 apples
1 tbsp raw coconut oil, liquefied
2 tsp cinnamon

Method:
Preheat the oven to 325 °F | 170 °C | Gas mark 3
Core, de-seed and cut the apples into thin slices or use a mandolin.
Add the apples to a large food plastic bag and add the coconut oil, cinnamon and shake until all the apples are coated well.
Place the apples on oil brushed or lined baking tray and bake for 30-35 minutes, turning over half way through the cooking time.
Leave to cool completely before storing in a paper bag or airtight container.

Tip: Use a dehydrator if you have one. Set to 125° for 7-8 hours.
Note: To add a variety of nutrition experiment with other ingredients too, like bananas, beetroot or parsnips.

Flea Free Dog Biscuits

Everyone dislikes sharing their home with fleas and these biscuits will encourage fleas to jump elsewhere, plus being delicious at the same time.

Ingredients:
2 cups organic rye flour
½ cup chick peas, cooked
1 tsp yeast extract with B12, no salt
1 clove garlic, minced
1 tbsp hemp oil
1 cup vegetable stock, see recipe in section 'How to Cook the Basics'

Method:
Preheat the oven to 375 °F | 190 °C | Gas mark 5.
Add the chick peas to a food processor and pulse until a coarse texture.
Add the rest of the ingredients and blend to form dough.
Roll out the dough to 1 cm thick and cut out rounds with your chosen cookie cutter.
Place the rounds on a lined baking sheet and bake in the oven for 25 minutes, until golden brown. Remove from the oven and place on a wire rack.
Leave to cool completely before storing in a paper bag or airtight container for up to 5 days.

Tip: If you do not have a cookie cutter use a pizza slicer or pasta roller to form shapes.
Note: For a wheat free and gluten free option use quinoa flour, which provides a good source of vegetable protein.

Coconut & Nut Butter Treats

Coconut has a variety of health benefits for dogs and they simply love it, whether it in oil form or just enjoying chewing on a piece of raw coconut.

Ingredients:
2 Flax 'eggs', see recipe in 'How to Cook the Basics'
Dry ingredients
1 cup organic rye flour
½ cup rolled oats
1 tsp carob powder
Wet ingredients
¼ cup raw organic peanut butter
¼ cup apple sauce, see recipe in 'How to Cook the Basics'
2 tbsp coconut oil
¼ cup coconut water

Method:
Preheat the oven to 375 °F | 190 °C | Gas mark 5.
Prepare the flax 'eggs' and leave in the fridge.
Add the dry ingredients to a large bowl and mix well.
In a separate bowl combine the wet ingredients and the flax eggs mixing in well.
Add the wet ingredients to the dry ingredients and stir to form dough.
Turn out the dough onto a lightly floured surface and roll out to your desired thickness then cut out rounds with a cookie cutter and place on a lightly coconut oiled or lined baking tray and bake for 10 minutes.
Leave to cool completely before storing in a paper bag or airtight container for up to 5 days.

Tip: If you do not have coconut water then use filtered water.
Note: Two heaped dessert spoonfuls of milled organic flaxseed provides 6.6g protein. Protein contributes to the growth and maintenance of muscle mass and the maintenance of normal bones.

Quinoa & Courgette Cookies

These treats are ideal for dogs that are on a grain free diet. Quinoa is classified as a seed which contains nine essential amino acids, including lysine and isoleucine acids.

Ingredients:
1 cup oat flour
2 tbsp flaxseed meal
1 tsp carob powder, optional
1 cup quinoa, cooked
1 cup courgette, grated
2 tbsp coconut oil, liquefied

Method:
Preheat the oven to 375 °F | 190 °C | Gas mark 5.
To a large bowl add oat flour, flaxseed meal and carob powder (if using) and stir.
Add the cooked quinoa and mix until well coated before adding the grated courgette and coconut oil, mixing together well.
On a lined baking sheet add a spoonful of mixture and repeat until you have a sheet of cookies. Bake in the oven for 20-25 minutes or until golden brown.
Remove from the oven and leave to cool on a wire wrack.
Store in a paper bag or airtight container for up to 5 days.

Tip: Add chia, pumpkin or hemp seeds to add more of a crunch.
Note: Carob naturally contains vitamins A, B, B1, B2, B3, B6 and D, calcium, iron, magnesium and potassium.

Coconut & Cinnamon Cookies

These are great to use as training treats because they are packed with energy, simply make them bite size to suit your dog. Also great to crumble into porridge to add a bit of nutritional boosting crunch.

Ingredients:
1 cup desiccated coconut
½ cup organic sunflower seeds
¼ cup rye flour
¼ cup black-strap molasses
1 flax egg, see recipe in 'How to Cook the Basics'
¼ cup raw coconut oil, liquefied
1 tsp cinnamon

Method:
Preheat the oven to 375 °F | 190 °C | Gas mark 5.
Add the coconut and sunflower seeds to a food blender and pulse until ground.
Then add the flour, molasses, flax egg, liquefied coconut oil, cinnamon and process until well combined.
Take a teaspoon sized amount of mixture and place on a lined baking sheet.
Bake for 10-15 minutes, or until golden brown.
Leave to cool completely before storing in a paper bag or airtight container.

Tip: If you don't have any flax eggs substitute with 2 tbsp of chick pea flour.
Note: Add dried cranberries to add vitamin C plus excellent for kidney and bladder health.

Savoury Bites

These savoury bites are great if you want to introduce more flavours to your dog's lifestyle. Use a pizza cutter to design your own bespoke treats.

Ingredients:
1 cup brown rice flour
2 tbsp ground flaxseed
2 tbsp fresh mint
1 tbsp fresh parsley
1 cup rolled oats
1 cup silken tofu
¼ cup peanut butter, see recipe in section 'How to Cook the Basics'

Method:
Preheat the oven to 375 °F | 190 °C | Gas mark 5.
In a large bowl, mix together the dry ingredients until well combined.
In a food processor blend the tofu and peanut butter until smooth.
Fold the tofu mixture into the dry ingredients a little at a time until well combined.
With a damp hand, lightly knead the dough until it forms dough.
Turn out the dough onto a lined baking tray, cover with a piece of parchment paper and roll out until ½ inch thick or your desired thickness.
Cut out 1 inch squared pieces with a knife or pizza cutter and bake for 10 minutes until firm.
Turn off the heat and leave the tray in the oven to allow the treats to cool and harden.
Leave to cool completely before storing in a paper bag or airtight container for up to 5 days.

Tip: Use cling film to roll out the mixture if you do not have parchment paper.
Note: Rice flour is a good alternative for dogs who are sensitive to wheat products.

Sweet Potato & Pineapple Treats

If you want to make these treats wheat free use brown rice flour. Any dog friendly flour works well with this recipe, so use what you have to hand.

Ingredients:
1 cup flour
½ cup rolled oats
1 sweet potato, cooked & mashed
½ cup pineapple purée

Method:
Preheat the oven to 375 °F | 190 °C | Gas mark 5.
Add the flour and oats to a large mixing bowl and stir together.
Add the mashed sweet potato and pineapple purée and mix to form dough.
Turn out the dough onto a lightly floured surface and roll out to ½ inch thick.
Cut out rounds with your favourite cookie cutter and place on a lined baking tray.
Bake for 10-15 minutes until lightly brown.
Leave to cool completely before storing in a paper bag or airtight container for up to 5 days.

Tip: If you do not have a cookie cutter roll the mixture into balls instead.
Note: Oats are low in gluten, cholesterol lowering and good for treating a wide variety of diseases in dogs, including inflammatory conditions.

Tahini Protein Balls

Tahini is a thick paste made from ground sesame seeds. It is more cost effective to make your own rather than buying it, especially if you use this ingredient regularly. These tahini protein balls should be given as treats straight from the freezer, however, if your dog has sensitive or weak teeth then omit this recipe or be cautious and make the balls smaller.

Ingredients:
½ cup tahini
1 small banana, mashed
1 cup rolled oats, toasted
1 tbsp nutritional yeast
1 tsp cinnamon

Method:
Mix the tahini and banana in a bowl until well combined.
Add the rest of the ingredients until a sticky mixture is formed. (If the mixture is too wet add more oats).
Take a small amount of dough and roll into balls with your hands, make each ball depending on your dogs jaw size.
Place each ball in an airtight container making sure there is a slight gap between each ball.
Store in the freezer for up to 3 months.

Tip: You can substitute the banana with another wet ingredient such as puréed pumpkin.
Note: Sesame seeds are good sources of copper, manganese, calcium, magnesium, iron, phosphorus, vitamin B1, and dietary fibre.

Parsley & Mint Breath Treats

Even vegan dogs are known for having slightly bad breath at times! These delicious treats with added parsley and mint will help to reduce intestinal gas production, induce fresh breath and boosts the immune system.

Ingredients:
1 ½ cups chickpea flour
½ cup organic rolled oats
1 tbsp flaxseed meal
1 tsp dried parsley
1 tsp dried mint
½ tsp spirulina powder, optional
½ cup filtered water

Method:
Preheat the oven to 375 °F | 190 °C | Gas mark 5.
In a large bowl stir together the dry ingredients and then mix in the water to form firm dough, knead with your hands if easier.
Turn out the dough onto parchment paper and roll out until 1cm thick.
Use a bone shape cutter to cut out rounds then transfer to a lined baking sheet and bake for 15-20 minutes.
Leave to cool completely before storing in a paper bag or airtight container for up to 5 days.

Tip: For a gourmet treat omit the water and replace with 1 cup of silken tofu.
Note: Make your own chickpea flour by milling dried chickpeas in a grinder.

Kidney Bean Bites

These super healthy treats are full of goodness. Make each bite as large or small as you like depending on the size of the treat you wish to bake for your dog.

Ingredients:
2 cups red kidney beans, cooked & rinsed
¼ cup vegetable stock, see recipe in section 'How to Cook the Basics'
2 tbsp apple purée, see recipe in section 'How to Cook the Basics'
2 cups organic rye flour
½ cup of chia seeds, milled
1 tsp fennel seeds, milled

Method:
Preheat the oven to 375 °F | 190 °C | Gas mark 5.
Add the kidney beans, vegetable stock and apple purée to a food processor and pulse until well combined, then transfer to a large mixing bowl.
Add the remaining ingredients to the wet mixture and fold in until well combined.
Take a teaspoon size amount of the mixture and place on a lined baking sheet.
Bake in the oven for 20 minutes or until lightly brown.
Leave to cool completely before storing in a paper bag or airtight container for up to 5 days.

Tip: Try aniseed powder instead of fennel seeds for a change of flavour.
Note: Kidney beans are excellent in helping your dog maintain a healthy heart.

Crunchy Wholemeal Toasty Treats

When I have left over bread this is a great crunchy treat to use up any surplus. If you have a large amount of leftover bread then make breadcrumbs and freeze until required.

Ingredients:
1 slice of wholemeal bread, home-made if possible
1 tbsp dog friendly oil

Method:
Preheat the oven to 375 °F | 190 °C | Gas mark 5.
Cut the bread into 1 inch squares and place in a plastic bag.
Pour over the oil and shake until the bread is coated well.
Bake on a lined baking sheet for 5-8 minutes until brown and crunchy.
Leave to cool completely before storing in a paper bag or airtight container.

Tip: Sprinkle these toasty treats over any meal to add a crunchy bite.
Note: Flaxseed oil is especially rich in omega-3 fatty acids.

Bulgur and Butter Bean Treats

My dogs love butter beans and this easy treat recipe incorporates lots of tasty flavours.

Ingredients:
3 cups flour
2 cups bulgur wheat, cooked
1 cup butter beans
1 cup polenta
3 cups warm vegetable stock, see recipe in section 'How to Cook the Basics'
1 tbsp sunflower seeds

Method:
Preheat the oven to 375 °F | 190 °C | Gas mark 5.
Mix the flour, bulgur wheat and polenta. Add 2 cups warm vegetable stock & mix well with your hands until dough is stiff, adding more stock as necessary.
Once the dough comes together, knead it for about 5-10 minutes then cover with cling-film and allow to rest for 10 minutes in the fridge.
On a lightly floured surface roll out the dough to ½ inch thickness.
Cut out treats using a cookie cutter or pizza cutter.
Place each treat on a lined baking sheet & bake for 20-25 minutes, until golden brown.
Turn off the oven & leave on the lowest shelf to harden.
Leave to cool completely before storing in a paper bag or airtight container.

Tip: Brush each treat with dairy free milk & dust with sesame seeds.
Note: Bulgur wheat is rich in protein and minerals and has a nutty taste.

Gingerbread Bones

If you do not have a bone cookie cutter then simply use any other you have or use a pasta or pizza cutter to make your own bespoke gingerbread treats.

Ingredients:
3 cups brown rice flour
½ tsp ground ginger
½ tsp ground cinnamon
¼ cup vegetable oil
¼ cup filtered water

Method:
Preheat the oven to 375 °F | 190 °C | Gas mark 5.
Mix all the dry ingredients together.
Add the vegetable oil and water and mix well until combined.
Turn out onto a lightly floured surface and roll out to ½ inch thickness.
Cut out your bone shapes and place on a lined baking tray and bake in the oven for 15-20 minutes until firm.
Leave to cool completely before storing in a paper bag or airtight container.

Tip: Leave the dough to rest for 20 minutes before rolling out.
Note: Cinnamon can aid in the treatment of a variety of medical issues including diabetes, arthritis, and infections.

Coconut & Peanut Cookies

This recipe started out as large cookies for me to dunk in my tea, but soon the dogs came sniffing around and asked for a bite, so I condensed down the size and slightly adjusted the ingredients. Nuts should be given in moderation to dogs but if you are in doubt, leave it out!

Ingredients:
¼ cup dairy-free milk
¼ cup organic black-strap molasses
½ cup peanut butter
½ cup desiccated coconut
1 tbsp dog carob drops, optional
2 cups flour
1 cup fine ground oats

Method:
Preheat the oven to 375 °F | 190 °C | Gas mark 5.
Add the milk, peanut butter, molasses and coconut to a large bowl and mix well.
If you are using carob drops add to the wet mixture and stir through.
Next add the ground oats and sift the flour into the mixture and fold to form sticky dough.
Using a cookie scoop, drop individual cookies onto a lined baking sheet & bake for 10 minutes.
Leave to cool completely on the baking tray before storing in a paper bag or airtight container.

Tip: If you want to be a little more experimental, try using crushed Cornflakes, Weetabix or Rice Krispies instead of the ground oats.
Note: Black strap molasses is a fabulous source of iron and B vitamins.

Cinnamon Muffins

We all like to impress our friends with our baking abilities and these make great birthday cakes; if you like you can ice them too and give them as gifts. Simply mix up ½ cup of plain soy yoghurt with 1 tbsp peanut butter and spread thinly.

Ingredients:
1 banana
1 tsp ground cinnamon
½ cup courgette, grated
¼ cup sunflower oil
¼ cup coconut flakes
1 tsp apple cider vinegar
1 ¼ cups wholemeal flour

Method:
Preheat the oven to 375 °F | 190 °C | Gas mark 5.
In a food processor add the courgette, banana and cinnamon pulse until puréed.
Add the sunflower oil and the coconut flakes and pulse again.
Add the rest of the ingredients and blend until the consistency of a smooth cake batter. Spoon the mixture into individual muffin cases until almost full.
Bake in the oven for 20-25 until the tops are golden. Test with a toothpick to see if it comes out clean, if so the muffins are done.
Leave to cool completely on a wire rack before storing in an airtight container for up to 5 days.

Tip: As an alternative to wholemeal use brown rice flour.
Note: Courgettes are a good source of vital nutrients including potassium and vitamin C.

Ice Pops

Ice pops are a great treat for dogs, especially in the summer months when it can be hot and can bring relief to dogs that have sore gums. Homemade fresh variations can be poured into an ice cube tray, rubber moulds or Kongs®. Simply freeze overnight then place the casing in warm water to release the pops and let your dog enjoy.

Serving options:

Fruit smoothies - blend fruit with vegan yoghurt

Blended vegetables - add 1 tbsp stock to 1 cup of vegetables then blend

Fruit purée - blend fruits together with raw coconut oil

Butter - Add peanut butter, mashed banana and apple purée then blend together

Vegan wet dog food - add to chosen receptacle for freezing

Tip: If you need to reuse the ice cube tray, pop out the cubes and store them in a Ziploc bag or airtight container in the freezer.
Note: The nutritional value list is endless; experiment with vegan canine friendly foods that your dog loves.

FAST FOOD IDEAS

Dogs love crunchy things and it's good to see them masticate fruit and vegetables themselves rather than having to mulch them down for them. I give my dogs a whole carrot or celery stick because it's more fun for them. These instant snack ideas with these healthy options straight from your fridge or vegetable rack. Just wash well, cut out any core or pips and let your dog munch away!

Carrot | Celery | Apple | Banana | Strawberry | Broccoli | Green leafy veg | Chick peas | Pear | Cucumber | Peas |

Dried Fruit

Dried fruit makes for a healthy and tasty snack. The best way to dry fruits is by using a dehydrator at a low temperature so the nutrients aren't destroyed by the cooking stage; this way you are getting the most out of your fruit. Those of you that have a dehydrator will know how to use this rather handy gadget, so for those of you that only have a good old fashioned oven here is an easy recipe for everyone. Dried fruit is also another easy fast treat for when you are out and about on walks or use as training treats; just cut them up into smaller pieces. Why not try and dry your own fruit.

First choose your fruit, make sure it is organic, washed and ripe enough to eat raw, rather than over ripe. Choose from a few options below

Apples | Bananas | Blackberries | Blueberry |Strawberry | Pears | Mango

Place slices of your chosen fruit on parchment lined baking trays, making sure the pieces of fruit aren't touching each other. Place the trays of fruit into a pre heated oven on 90°F to 150°F. Whilst the fruit is drying out resist all urges to turn up the heat, you do not want to cook the fruit, just dehydrate it. After 2 hours turn the fruit over for another 2 hours, then test the fruit every 30 minutes thereafter to see if the fruit is chewy, but still pliable.

When the fruit is ready, remove from the oven and let dried fruit sit out overnight (at least 12 hours) before storing in glass or plastic containers to "cure." Leave the container open for 4-5 days so that any moisture left from the drying process can evaporate. Shake the container every day or so to move the fruit around. Seal the containers after 5 days and enjoy dried fruits until next harvest season, about 10 months.

It may be quite time consuming, but you'll have some fantastic, healthy dried fruit perfect for treats. Remember, currants and raisins are toxic to dogs.

KONG® FILLED TREAT IDEAS

Treat dispensing toys are an ideal way to ease boredom for dogs, whilst also reducing the risk of destructive behaviour when left alone. A bored dog will find something to do (usually involving your furniture or other treasured belongings!), so helping your dog to work off their mental energy can work wonders.
Kong toys are such a great idea and founded by Joe Markham. His inspiration to find an indestructible toy for his retired police dog has been a must have toy for dogs all around the world. Dogs love to chew and Kongs are great for all kinds of boredom busters! Simply fill the Kong with yummy goodies and watch your dog have lots of fun. If you are going out for a short while pre freeze a filled Kong in advance so that whilst you are out your dog is entertained for longer. (Always make sure that you have the right size Kong before leaving your dog unattended.)

Savoury

- Plain soya yoghurt, mashed ripe banana and peanut butter
- Sweet potatoes mashed mixed with nutritional yeast
- Cooked rice mashed with marmite and frozen
- Home made hummus
- Pumpkin purée
- Mashed pea & mint
- Tofu yoghurt with mint, parsley & spirulina
- Cooked broccoli and carrot mashed
- Cooked chickpeas mashed
- Any meal (puréed)

Sweet

- Melon, strawberry and banana whizzed up in a blender
- Stewed apple, agave nectar and mashed banana
- Dip fruit such as strawberries in soy yoghurt & freeze for instant treats
- Purée banana, blueberries and strawberries and freeze
- Mix silken tofu with mango then freeze
- With peach or fruit small chunks including purée
- Mix tofu yoghurt with puréed fruit then freeze
- Purée watermelon and mint then freeze
- Kale and berries whizzed up in a blender
- Mix coconut milk with fruit and freeze

HOMEMADE REMEDIES

Most over the counter flea products contain pesticides, permethrin, organophosphates and other toxic ingredients linked with thousands of pet deaths and diseases. Most importantly no-one knows the long term effects these harsh chemicals have on our pets' health. Fleas and other parasites become increasingly resistant to the synthetic chemicals man has produced for their control. Pesticide manufacturers are making their products increasingly stronger — and more dangerous — in an attempt to keep pace with the parasites. Making your own not only ensures that your dog and home is protected against fleas, also it is quite satisfying to know that you are using ingredients that are not intrusively harmful and that have not been tested on animals. Many natural and herbal off the shelf flea and tick products contain an ingredient called Neem oil; whilst it is very effective it can be rather pungent. There are several ingredients that naturally repel fleas and ticks, such as cedarwood, eucalyptus, tea tree oil, citronella or lavender. You can use any of these ingredients to incorporate into your own home made sprays. I have tried quite a number of flea repellents and this one below I find not only works the best but smells divine too.

Homemade Flea Shampoo

Ingredients:
1 cup of unscented vegan baby shampoo
1 tsp apple cider vinegar
2 drops of lemon oil
2 drops of lavender oil

Method:
Mix all of the ingredients together and decant into a sterilised squeeze bottle. Use as you would a normal shampoo and store in a cool dry cupboard for up to 3 months.

Flea & Tick Repellent Spray

Ingredients:
1 lemon, un-waxed
1 handful of fresh rosemary leaves, roughly chopped
1 tbsp of apple cider vinegar
1 cup of water
5 drop of tea tree oil

Method:
Grate the rind off the lemon, extract the juice and add to a saucepan together with the rosemary and water. Bring to a near boil and simmer for a few minutes, add the apple cider vinegar and then transfer to an air tight container and leave to infuse overnight. Strain off the liquid into a sterilised trigger spray bottle and add the tea tree oil. Shake well and label the spray bottle and store out of reach of doggies.

Application:
Spray your dog as and when required; rub over the coat and skin paying attention to the base of the tail area, behind the ears, belly area and leg creases to make sure you treat the areas where fleas like to nest. It is important to remember this is a topical spray and is never to be ingested.

INGREDIENTS & THEIR NUTRITIONAL VALUES

Fresh organic fruits and vegetables are fundamental to a dog's diet. They are packed full of essential nutrients that offer a variety of health benefits including antioxidant, anti-inflammatory and liver health promoting activities. The vibrant colours of fruit and vegetables tell us which important disease fighting phytonutrients they contain. Phytonutrients are powerful antioxidants that are indicated by the colours of fruit and vegetables. They work synergistically with one another as do vitamins, minerals, and enzymes. Tens of thousands of known phytonutrients have been studied so far, and more are explored every day. To get a good balance of phytonutrients, dogs should consume fruits and vegetables from the entire colour spectrum. The colour of fruits and vegetables makes a difference because the pigments that produce colours are also the phytonutrients. Antioxidants including vitamins A, C, D and E, selenium, bioflavinoids from vegetables (e.g. red bell peppers, broccoli, Brussels sprouts, spinach), fruits (e.g. blueberries, cranberries, pomegranate) and herbs (e.g. oregano, garlic, turmeric) can be used as bio-support to strengthen the dogs' metabolism and immune system.

Green fruit and vegetables contain flavonoids, lutein, indoles and chlorophyll which together may help age related macular degeneration, boost the immune system and help protect against cellular damage. Plus most green vegetables such as spinach, kale and collard greens are considered super foods because they contain a high amount of antioxidants. Plenty of vitamin A, C and E can be found in most green foods, in addition to other important nutrients such as iron and zinc. Green foods suitable for dogs include kale, spinach, rocket, lettuce, watercress, cucumber, broccoli, brussels sprouts, cabbage, pak choi, spring greens, green beans, peas, sugar snap peas, mange tout, courgette, green pepper and green apples.

Red fruit and vegetables get their colour from lycopene and anthocyanins which together may help protect against cancer and heart disease. Red foods suitable for dogs include tomatoes, guava, watermelon, raspberries, cranberries, strawberries, apples, red plums and red peppers.

Blue or purple fruit and vegetables get their colour from anthocyanins which belong to a larger family of phytochemicals called flavonoids. Rich in antioxidant and anti-inflammatory properties. Blue or purple foods suitable for dogs include blueberries, blackberries, red cabbage, beetroot, blackcurrants, purple plums and aubergine.

Yellow or orange fruit and vegetables get their colour from carotenoids; alpha-carotene, beta carotene and beta cryptoxanthin converting them into Vitamin A in the body. Together they aid good vision, normal growth and development, a strong immune system and to keep the skin and cells healthy.

Yellow or orange foods suitable for dogs include carrots, winter squash, papaya, apricots, cantaloupe and gala melon, mangoes, nectarines, peaches, pineapple, passion fruit, swede, sweet potatoes, butternut squash, pumpkin, yellow and orange peppers and sweet corn.

White fruit and vegetables get their colour from anthoxanthins; the most common is quercetin, which research suggests may lower the risk of heart disease, plus helping to ease the symptoms of allergies, it also contains anti inflammatory properties. White foods suitable for dogs include bananas, cauliflower, celery, garlic, parsnips and turnips.

New experimental studies are emerging that demonstrate multiple effects of fruits and vegetables, which suggests that they actually have an even greater role to play in canine health than already positive results seen to date. Certain seeds, grains and lentils explode with nutrition when they germinate and are beneficial to canine health. Having a balance of calcium, phosphorous, protein and amino acids is essential to a vegan lifestyle so try to make sure that all of these elements are met by giving a wide variety of foods. As my 94 year old gran always says 'everything in moderation. This is a great way to think in regards to what foods to give your dog on a daily basis. Think variety, think moderation, think nutritional value and think balance. So dogs go and eat your veggies!

Fruit

All dogs love something sweet and many love fruit whether it is fresh, frozen or dried. I like to have dried pieces of fruit when we are out on walks so that we can all share a treat or two for an energy boost which is a natural source of potassium. Fruits are vital for adding vitamins, minerals, fibre and energy, best eaten fresh or frozen to ensure the nutrients are intact. The natural colouring of red fruits is called lycopene and anthocyanin which contain phytochemical a natural disease fighter, so incorporating red sustenances such as strawberries, apples, watermelon and cranberries may help to reduce diseases, such as diabetes, heart disease and high cholesterol. Rich, flavourful fruits are densely packed with nutrients that act as medicine as well as food and can be fed as treats, or sprinkled over or mixed into your dog's food. A large portion of calories in fruit come from sugar so make sure that you add variety as well as extra nutrition and taste to your dogs diet. **NB:** It is important to mention again that you should never allow your dog to eat any of the seeds, stems or stones from any fruit since they may be toxic in large amounts, and make sure that you don't feed your dog fruit too close to a high-protein meal for optimum digestion. Also, if you suspect your dog has a food allergy of any type, consult your veterinarian.

Apple – With so many varieties to choose from apples are high in fibre, vitamins A and C, omega 3 and 6, antioxidants, flavonoids and polyphenols. Complex carbohydrates help maintain a steady blood sugar level and because of their pectin value apples are considered good for the heart. The skin of an apple contains high levels of vitamin A and pectin, a fibre that can improve digestion by strengthening intestinal muscles. Apples are the base of apple cider vinegar which is a must have ingredient for your pantry. If your dog doesn't like raw apple then see my recipe for apple purée which can be added to meals or treats.

Apricot – My dogs love dried apricots which I feed as a treat on walks as an energy boost. Only buy 100% pure organic dried apricots that are naturally dark in colour, the dried bright orange apricots have been modified with sulphur which is bad for dogs and us. Apricots are an excellent source of vitamin A (from beta-carotene) vitamin C and potassium.

Banana – Good source of vitamin B6 as well as vitamin C, potassium, phosphorous, magnesium. In a recent study, researchers found that fresh bananas protected the animals' stomachs from wounds. Bananas are good with rice or oatmeal to soothe a dog's upset stomach.

Blackberry – Very nutritious and packed with antioxidants to fight free radicals. Good sources of antioxidants (anthocyanins), polyphenols, tannin, fibre, manganese, folate and omega-3. High in vitamins C, K, A and E. Try and allow your dog to eat blackberries straight from the bush when in season so they can forage for their own food.

Blueberry – Boasting one of the highest antioxidant capacities among all fruits and vegetables, blueberries have powerful health supportive properties so a super nutritious snack for dogs. Full of vitamin K, C, manganese and fibre which helps heart function as well as lower the risk of stroke. Proven to help with memory and nerve cell protection these blueberries are vital for senior dogs. Eaten fresh or frozen it doesn't matter as the nutritional value remains equal.

Coconut – Coconut contains albumin, which is good for red blood formation. Coconut is also rich in fibre with its digestible oils and said to aid in removing worm eggs. The great thing about coconut is that you can be sure there are no pesticides because of the hard exterior of the shell. Research has now shown that coconut oil is a healthy saturated fat that supports the immune system function. Raw coconut oil contains lauric acid, which has antiviral, antibacterial and antifungal properties and is easily absorbed and digested.

Cranberry - Cranberries are well-documented for their ability to improve urinary health in both humans and animals because they contain a natural medicinal compound that prevents bacteria from clinging to the walls of the bladder, urethra and kidneys to maintain a healthy urinary pH. Dried cranberries are good for a treat now and again.

Dates (pitted) – Extremely rich in folic acid which is an important B vitamin necessary for growth, liver and glands. Folic acid helps the formation of red blood cells so great for dogs with anaemia. Dates are also rich in minerals like calcium, manganese, copper, and magnesium. Calcium is an important mineral that is an essential constituent of bone and teeth, and required by the body for muscle contraction, blood clotting, and nerve impulse conduction.

Fig - Figs can have a lot of health benefits for dogs since they contain nutrients such as natural sugars, potassium and fibre. They can definitely be a good source of energy.

Mango - An excellent source of vitamin A, potassium, vitamin B6, vitamin C, vitamin E, and flavonoids like beta-carotene and alpha-carotene.

Melon – There are quite a few varieties of melon and dogs love them all, especially mashed up or puréed to make a frozen ice pop treat in the summer.

Watermelon includes flavonoids, carotenoids, and triterpenoids, has anti-inflammatory and antioxidant health benefits. Cantaloupe is good for both vitamin C and vitamin A, great for potassium and a good source of B vitamins (B1, B3, B6, and folate) as well as vitamin K, magnesium and fibre.

Pear – Like apples, pears contain pectin which helps strengthen the intestines. Pears are also good sources of potassium, a nutrient that aids in maintaining heart and muscle strength as well as nerve transmission and carbohydrate metabolism. The fibre found in pears promotes colon health so can be particularly good for dogs who suffer from constipation or irregularity. The fibre found in pears promotes colon health.

Pineapple – Pineapple can be a good food therapy for helping allergies and are good sources of vitamin C, B6, and B1. Frozen chunks of pineapple can be a fun summer treat. It is said that pineapple can help stop coprophagia (eating faeces).

Raspberry – Raspberries are a good source of dietary fibre, antioxidants, potassium, manganese, copper, iron, magnesium, whilst also rich in vitamin C, K and B-complex. It is said that the raspberry leaf smoothes muscles such as the uterus and so helps ensure an easy and straightforward delivery.

Strawberry – With all the antioxidants and anti inflammatory properties strawberries are said to be the best fruit source for vitamin C and a nutritional powerhouse for dogs. Also boasting dietary fibre as well as Manganese, Iodine and Folate, plus Vitamin B6 and Omega 3 fats. Studies suggest that strawberries contain an enzyme called malic acid that may help whiten your dog's teeth.

Vegetables

Vegetables are a great way to incorporate all the essential nutrients including vitamins and minerals, antioxidants, phytochemicals, enzymes as well as the all important fibres into your dog's diet. So your dog absorbs all of the nutritional goodness make sure they are chopped, grated or puréed, either cooked, steamed or raw. Green leafy vegetables get their dark colour from chlorophyll which helps replenish red blood cells which aids in cleansing all the cells of the body, fight infection, heal wounds, build the immune system and detoxify all systems, particularly the liver. It also promotes digestive health which is why many dogs with acute digestive problems tend to eat grass. Orange and yellow vegetables such as sweet potatoes, carrots, cantaloupe melon and winter squash are loaded with potassium, beta-carotene and vitamin C which are great for aiding healing of the skin and many people believe is good for vision, not to mention adding magnesium and calcium, which is essential for strong bones.

Asparagus – Good source of folate, potassium and vitamin C. Is also provides useful amounts of vitamins E and K, and some B vitamins (thiamin and niacin), plus some minerals, including phosphorous, zinc and manganese.

Beetroot – Beetroot provide antioxidant, anti-inflammatory, and detoxification support. Beets are high in nutrients and low in calories. Grate raw beets onto meals to get the best nutritional value.

Bell Pepper – Are good in B-complex group of vitamins such as niacin, pyridoxine (vitamin B-6), riboflavin, and thiamin (vitamin B-1). It is suggested that the beta carotene found in green peppers can help prevent cancer. It is also linked to a reduction of cataracts and other eye issues within ageing dogs. Furthermore, studies have led researchers to believe that beta carotene can also help prevent arthritis in dogs.

Broccoli - Broccoli is an excellent food for dogs because it does not raise blood glucose levels. In addition to vitamins A, C, D and beta carotene, broccoli contains folic acid, fibre, chromium and calcium. Research suggests that 33 cancer-preventing compounds are found in broccoli. Completely safe in quantities not exceeding 10% of daily intake.

Brussels Sprouts – Brussels sprouts are an excellent source of vitamins C, A , B1, B6 and K. Rich in minerals like copper, calcium, potassium, iron, manganese and phosphorus. Plus they are great for dietary fibre. Brussels sprouts also contain anti-oxidant properties, all of which help reduce inflammation and benefit blood health and circulation.

Butternut squash - Rich in B-complex group of vitamins like folates, riboflavin, niacin, vitamin B-6 (pyridoxine), thiamin, and pantothenic acid essential for the proper functioning of both the nervous and immune systems. Low in fat, butternut squash delivers an ample dose of dietary fibre, making it an exceptionally heart-friendly choice.

Cabbage – With so many varieties to choose from cabbage is a great source of phytonutrients and anti-oxidants. Also contains adequate amounts of minerals such as potassium, manganese, iron, and magnesium. Not only can cabbage aid with your dog's digestion, it is also good for the skin and coat.

Carrot – With vitamins A and C, carrots are also sources of vitamins D, E, K, riboflavin, niacin, calcium, potassium, phosphorous, sodium, magnesium and iron. These important vitamins and nutrients support the immune system and aid digestion. I like to use baby carrots because the smaller the carrot the more goodness they contain; also make sure that you use them as quickly as you can from the ground because sadly the goodness depletes as the hours go by.

Cauliflower - Cauliflower is an excellent source of vitamin C, vitamin K, folate, pantothenic acid, and vitamin B6. It is a very good source of choline, dietary fibre, omega-3 fatty acids, manganese, phosphorus, and biotin. Additionally, it is a good source of vitamin B2, protein, vitamin B1, niacin, and magnesium.

Celery - An excellent source of nutrients to improve heart health and reduce cancer rates. Celery is rich in calcium, potassium, phosphorous, sodium, iron, and vitamins A, B and C. Can help with arthritis or joint pain, good for flushing out toxins and aiding good kidney and urinary health, whilst also helping to support a healthy immune system. Celery is reputed to reduce nervousness in animals and act as an acid neutraliser.

Courgette - A good source of calcium, potassium, beta-carotene, and folate. In addition, they contain moderate levels of B-complex group of vitamins like thiamin, pyridoxine, riboflavin and minerals like iron, manganese, phosphorus, and zinc. Can also increase the health of your dog's skin and fur as well as help them lose weight.

Cucumber - Phytonutrients found in cucumber provides valuable antioxidant and anti-inflammatory benefits. Combine with carrots to promote a healthy liver and kidneys. Cucumber is a great raw treat for dogs that love to crunch, fat free too so good for overweight dogs or those that are obsessed with food.

Garlic (fresh) – Whilst many people believe that garlic is toxic for dogs it is actually beneficial to dogs in reasonable quantities. People believe garlic is toxic because it is closely related to the onion which contains thiosulphate. Garlic is high in vitamins, minerals and nutrients and is also a natural flea repellent and de-wormer. Has anti-bacterial or anti-viral qualities so a good alternative to antibiotics. Omit garlic from recipes to puppies less that six months old.

Ginger (fresh) - has anti-inflammatory and antibacterial properties which are beneficial to help aid absorption of food, whilst boosting healthy blood circulation thus helping reduce the risk of heart disease. A great help to dogs that suffer from motion sickness. Ginger is also known to help with allergies.

Green Beans - Studies have also shown that green bean intake in animals can improve blood fat levels and protect against oxygen damage, plus they are low in calories. Green beans also contain omega-3 fatty acids, which also contribute to the cardiovascular benefits. Green beans are a great source of vitamins A, C and K, as well as calcium, copper, fibre, folic acid, iron, niacin, manganese, potassium, riboflavin and thiamin.

Kale – Kale is a very versatile and nutritious green leafy vegetable, low in fat, no cholesterol but health benefiting anti-oxidant properties. Kale provides rich nutrition ingredients that offer protection from vitamin A deficiency, osteoporosis, iron-deficiency anaemia, and believed to protect from cardiovascular diseases. Packed full of essential minerals and vitamins which boost the immune system. A dark green leafy vegetable with Vitamin A and C kale is fantastic for the skin and has been known to slow down premature ageing.

Kelp – A type of sea vegetable, great source of minerals, such as magnesium, iron, potassium and iodine. Contains minerals, amino acids, simple and complex carbohydrates, Iodine and Calcium.

Lettuce – There are many varieties of lettuce all packed with essential nutrients that benefit canine health. Lettuce leaves are one of the very low calorie green vegetables and are the store house of many phytonutrients that have health promoting and disease prevention properties.

Parsnip - Very low in Saturated Fat, Cholesterol and Sodium. It is also a good source of dietary fibre, Vitamin C, Folate and Manganese. In addition, it also has healthy levels of minerals like iron, calcium, copper, potassium, manganese and phosphorus. Potassium is an important component of cell and body fluids that helps control heart rate and blood pressure by countering effects of sodium.

Peas – There are many varieties of peas and they are all healthy and nutritious for dogs. Green peas are one of the most nutritious leguminous vegetables rich in health benefiting phytonutrients, minerals, vitamins and antioxidants.

Potatoes - Good source of vitamins C and B6, naturally low in fat. Baked or boiled and then mashed. However, poisonous alkaloids (solanine) are present in green sprouts and green potato skins.

Pumpkin – Pumpkin is loaded with vitamin A, anti-oxidants and is a rich source of fibre. Provides anti-inflammatory benefits, helps to regulate blood sugar levels and promotes cardiovascular health. If your dog is overweight then pumpkin is an excellent food to incorporate into meals because it gives animals the feeling of being full while being a low-calorie food, also a good remedy for upset tummies.

Soy Bean Edamame - Great source of protein, iron, fibre, vitamin K, Omega-3 fats, phosphorus, vitamin B2, potassium, copper and magnesium. Organic is best.

Spinach - Raw or cooked spinach are excellent sources of iron, containing twice as much as other leafy greens and contains a cross section of phytonutrients and antioxidants. Great for puppies this leafy green vegetable is also a good source of fibre, calcium, potassium, and vitamins A, B6 and K. Spinach is particularly good for dogs that need to ward off inflammatory and cardiovascular problems as well as cancer.

Squash - Winter squash is low in calories and a good source of fibre. Good source of vitamin A, vitamin C, potassium, folate, omega 3 fatty acids and vitamins B1, B3, B5 & B6. A very versatile vegetable which is also ideal to use in baking.

Sweet corn - Contains good levels of some of the valuable B-complex group of vitamins such as thiamin, niacin, pantothenic acid, folates, riboflavin, and pyridoxine. Many of these vitamins function as cofactors to enzymes during substrate metabolism. To maintain their goodness crush sweet corn before adding to meals.

Sweet potato – A highly nutritious source of carbohydrate, providing high sources of beta-carotene and potassium which helps aid recovery, so great for active dogs. Also rich in vitamin A, C, E and also manganese which are essential for healthy muscle function.

Swede - Low in Sodium, and low in Saturated Fat and Cholesterol. It is also a good source of Dietary Fibre, Thiamin, Vitamin B6, Calcium, Magnesium and Phosphorus, and a very good source of Vitamin C, Potassium and Manganese.

Turnip – A good source of calcium and folate and, best of all, they are low in calories. High in folic acid and Vitamin B6, both of which can be beneficial to dogs with renal disease. Turnips are high in water content and act as a natural diuretic as they help the kidneys create urine, thus stimulating natural kidney function.

Watercress – Dogs love the peppery and tangy flavour of cress which is a storehouse of many natural phytonutrients that have health promotional and disease prevention properties. High in Vitamins C, A, B-1, B-2, B-6, and K, as well as the minerals manganese, phosphorous, potassium, and calcium. Watercress is reported to have many health benefits including as a digestive aid and anti-inflammatory benefits.

Grains

Whole grains are inexpensive food sources which provide carbohydrates, vitamins and minerals. Studies have shown that combining grains has a superior protein balance of amino acids which is found to be more complete. Well cooked whole grains or whole wheat are good sources of protein and carbohydrates, as well as other nutrients such as B vitamins. I get asked quite a lot from people who are confused as to what a grain is and what is not, and what to feed their dog if they have food allergies. If your dog has a known allergy to grains then simply leave them out, there are plenty of other plant based ingredient options available. Always rinse grains thoroughly before and after cooking to remove toxins and debris. Whole grains (like barley and oats) provide a nutritionally rich source of fibre which is beneficial for digestive health without the detrimental effects on metabolism and weight gain. Not all grains are good and some dogs may well have problems digesting them especially if they have a delicate gut. Unless your dog requires a grain free diet for health reasons, well cooked grains are good sources of both protein and carbohydrates but on the whole they are a valuable source of nutrition. Some dogs can be allergic to wheat, so if your dog is one of these, try and source a wheat free option and the majority of dogs can digest and do love pasta.

Barley – Whole grain barley is low in fat and high in carbohydrate, has as a low glycemic index and high in soluble fibre, specifically beta-glucan. Barley is highest in fibre of all the whole grains, is high in antioxidants, vitamins and minerals.

Brown Rice – Naturally gluten free, with natural fibre for healthy digestion. A great source of manganese, brown rice also offers a source for magnesium and selenium. Brown rice is rich in antioxidants, promotes weight loss, and helps to stabilise blood sugar levels.

Buckwheat – Many people think buckwheat is a grain but it is actually a fruit seed so is a great option for dogs that have an allergy to grain products, is especially high in protein, and rich in the amino acid lysine. Rich in poly-unsaturated essential fatty acids, such as linoleic acid. Contains vitamins B1, C and E, plus has a higher level of zinc, copper, and manganese than other cereal grains. Energising and nutritious and can be served as an alternative to rice or made into porridge.

Bulgur - Bulgur is a whole grain pre cooked cracked wheat so very quick to prepare. Very low in saturated fat, cholesterol and sodium, also a very good source of fibre and manganese. Contains vitamins A, B3, folate, choline and betaine. Bulgur is high in iron, zinc, phosphorus and calcium whilst being cholesterol-free.

Corn – Though sometimes dismissed as a nutrient poor starch – both a second-rate vegetable and a second-rate grain – corn is currently being reassessed and now viewed as a healthy food. Dog friendly corn products include fresh corn on the cob, popcorn, polenta, corn muffins and flours.

Millet - An ancient grain used as a source of important nutrients, including copper, manganese, phosphorus, and magnesium. Rich in B vitamins, iron and potassium, whilst low in calories. Millet provides essential amino acids and is a good source of fibre. Highly nutritious, gluten free and beneficial to the stomach, spleen and pancreas. Millet lowers the glycemic index which allows the animal to utilise energy more evenly.

Oats - A great source of iron, manganese, zinc, and B vitamins. High in protein and soluble fibre called betaglucan found to be especially effective in lowering cholesterol. Oats are great for dogs and have many health benefits such as being a digestive aid to help calm the intestinal tract so a good addition to meals when changing over to a plant based lifestyle. Oats are inherently gluten-free, have anti-inflammatory and calming effects which soothes itchiness.

Pearl Barley – Is not a whole grain. Pearl barley has been polished, or "pearled" to remove some or the entire outer bran layer along with the hull. Although it is technically a refined grain, it's much healthier than other refined grains because (a) some of the bran may still be present and (b) the fibre in barley is distributed throughout the kernel, and not just in the outer bran layer. Pearl barley also cooks more quickly than whole grain barley.

Polenta - Polenta (corn or maize) contains traces of the minerals calcium, iron, magnesium, phosphorus, sodium and zinc. Generally lower in protein and has a lower vitamin and mineral content than other grains. High in potassium and low in sodium. Contains vitamin C, E and B-group vitamins such as thiamin, riboflavin, niacin, vitamin B6 (pyridoxine), folate and pantothenic acid. Polenta is a versatile food plus being gluten-free.

Rice - High in natural fibre and a good source of selenium, good for coat health and immune system. White rice is refined, with the germ and bran removed. Whole-grain rice is usually brown. Rice can be excellent for pups or dogs with digestive problems. All rice should be rinsed well before and after cooking.

Quinoa - One of the highest quality proteins on the planet. Technically a seed quinoa contains nine essential amino acids, is high in iron and calcium, and is a good source of manganese, magnesium and copper, as well as fibre. An excellent plant based ingredient for vegan dogs.

Legumes (pulses), Nuts and Seeds

Legumes (pulses) are an inexpensive source of dietary fibre & valuable protein which is fundamental for vegan dogs. Tempeh is a good vegan source of L-carnitine and a whole food soy product. Dogs love beans, lentils, split peas, chick peas and sprouting beans. Lentils in particular are a low glycemic food, nutrient and protein rich and a natural source of phytochemicals and antioxidants; lentils are ideal for dogs with food intolerances. All legumes should be well cooked until very soft and can also be mashed or puréed in a food processor.

Black eyed beans – Powerful fibre rich protein and antioxidants. Low in fat and sodium, saturated fat free, cholesterol free, an excellent source of vitamin B1 and a good source of fibre, magnesium, phosphorous and zinc.

Butter beans – Also known as lima beans, are a very good source of cholesterol-lowering fibre. When combined with whole grains such as rice, butter beans provide virtually fat free high quality protein meal. Good sources of copper, manganese, folate, phosphorus, potassium, iron and vitamin B1 and B6.

Chick Peas – Also known as garbanzo, are high in fibre, protein and important phytonutrients. Chick peas mashed make a good meal addition for puppies. Chick peas offer fibre that can ease canine constipation, as well as lecithin, potassium, and vitamins A, B and C. Good for active dogs as they boost energy because of their high iron content. They have a nut like taste and a firm buttery texture so good for adding to dogs meals that are changing over to a plant based diet.

Flaxseed / Linseed – Rich in omega-3 fatty acids, anti-oxidants, nutrients, minerals and vitamins that are essential for optimal health, whist being good sources of vitamins B and E, potassium, calcium, phosphorus, iron, magnesium and zinc. Omega-3 fatty acids, helps fatigue, dry skin, cracked nails, thin and breakable hair, constipation, immune system malfunction, aching joints, depression, arthritis, and hormone imbalances. Flax seeds also help pass toxins out of the body. Excellent source of fermentable and non-fermentable fibre; if you purchase flax or flaxseed you are almost certainly buying linseed or linseed oil. Recommended by vets to help with dry, flaky skin conditions.

Lentils – Red, green or brown these legumes are a staple larder ingredient because dogs love them, plus being excellent sources of nutrients and protein. Particularly good for active dogs as they enhance endurance and maintain blood glucose levels. Studies have proven that dogs fed lentils or peas compared to corn or rice have lower glucose and insulin levels. Lentils are an ideal ingredient for dogs with food intolerances.

Mung Bean – Mung bean sprouts can be eaten raw or cooked. Sprouts are a good source of iron, folate and vitamins K and C. Vitamin C is important in boosting the dog's immune system and folate is important for cell growth. Bean sprouts also contain enzymes that aid in the digestion of carbohydrates, protein and fat.

Pinto Beans – Pinto beans are the most non-allergenic food for vegan dogs. In addition to lowering cholesterol, pinto beans high fibre content prevents blood sugar levels from rising too rapidly after a meal, making these beans an especially good choice for dogs with diabetes. Pinto beans are also sources of molybdenum, folate, protein, vitamin B1, and vitamin B6 as well as the minerals copper, phosphorus, iron, magnesium, manganese and potassium.

Pumpkin seeds – Pumpkin seeds include important nutrients to your pet's overall good health. Full of manganese, phosphorous, copper, vitamin K, vitamin E, B vitamins such as thiamin, riboflavin, niacin, vitamin B-6, potassium, calcium, iron, magnesium, zinc and selenium. Pumpkin seeds contain the amino acid called cucurbitacin which paralyses and eliminates worms from the digestive tract so a great natural de-wormer for dogs.

Peanuts – Rich in protein, antioxidants, vitamin E and manganese. Peanuts also contain oleic acid, the healthy fat also found in olive oil.

Red Kidney Beans- Small red kidney beans have antioxidant properties, making them a good addition to your dog's diet as it helps lower cholesterol. Dogs can eat red kidney beans as it also helps maintenance of the colon with better bowel movement.

Sesame seeds – Full of essential minerals such as iron, phosphorus and calcium. The antioxidants in sesame seeds fight free radicals and help to strengthen the immune system.

Soy Bean – Soybean products are good protein sources for both adult and growing dogs. Research continues to show that soy products are a superb source of bodybuilding protein, coat nourishing vegetable oil and healthful fibre for dogs. High in vitamins and folic acid High in essential amino acids, good source of fatty acids, potassium and antioxidants. Aid good digestibility and is less allergenic for dogs than other protein sources such as meat and dairy products.

Sunflower seeds - Delicious and a super source of antioxidants and B complex vitamins.

Oils

When considering oils do check out their ingredient list to see where the fats and oils are coming from. Fats in dog foods are typically supplied by animal fat but also oils from plants. Quality vegan dog foods will list sources of fat that provide the suitable balance of omega-3 and omega-6 fatty acids. You can also make your own oils by adding various herbs and leave to infuse in a lovely glass jar and use when required. For maintaining bodily functions, fatty acids are important for dogs, providing energy, renew cells, nerves, muscles and other tissues. Fats also have a key role in absorbing certain fat soluble vitamins like A, D, E and K.

Note: The chemical composition of oil is also a key factor in the risk of rancidity. Here the basic principles involve saturated and unsaturated fat. The more saturated fat contained in oil, the less susceptible it is to rancidity. The greater the amount of unsaturated fat in an oil, the more likely it is to become rancidity. Since the healthiest plant oils are all highly unsaturated, they are especially susceptible to rancidity. In a case like flaxseed oil, where the chemical composition of the oil places it at great risk for rancidity, it's best to avoid any type of heating at temperatures above 150°F (66°C) and to store the oil in the refrigerator and add to meals just before feeding.

Coconut oil - Coconut oil is unique because it is composed predominantly of Medium Chain Triglycerides (MCT) which makes it different from all other fats and gives it its unique character and healing properties. MCT are easily absorbed, digested and nourish the body. Unlike other fats, they put little strain on the digestive system and provide a quick source of energy necessary to promote healing. Coconut oil gently elevates the metabolism, provides a higher level of energy and vitality, protects the body from illness, and speeds up the healing process. As a bonus, coconut oil improves the dog's skin and coat, reduces allergic reactions and prevents and treats yeast and fungal infections.

Flaxseed oil – Rich in omega 3, the essential fatty acids contained in flax seed oil ensure basic cellular health in all animals. Veterinarians have been recommending flax seed oil for dogs for quite some time. It has been reported to help with inflammatory disease, heart disease, blood pressure, kidney and artery function, cancer and allergies. Good for maintaining a healthy shiny coat.

Hemp Oil - Contains all the essential amino acids and essential fatty acids. Includes the perfect ratio of Omega 6 to Omega 3, all important fatty acids which dogs require. Hemp seed oil can enhance blood circulation in brains, thicken the fur texture, keep the skin less shedding whilst preventing dandruff.

Oregano oil - Studies have shown that oregano oil has antibacterial, antiviral, anti-parasitic and anti fungal properties. Has been proven to treat everything from arthritis and allergies to influenza, viruses, infections and wounds.

Olive oil - Rich in monounsaturated fats, olive oil prevents and lessens the effects of cardiovascular disease and diabetes. With high levels of antioxidants, including polyphenols, vitamin E, chlorophyll, and carotenoids. Olive oil is very effective at arming the dog's immune system so it can efficiently fight off disease.

Sunflower oil –Sunflower oil is pressed from sunflower seeds and is generally regarded as one of the healthier oils in dog foods. It is low in saturated fat and rich in the natural antioxidant vitamin E.

Vegetable oil - Vegetable oil contains omega-6 fatty acids, which help the dog's coat inside and out.

Milk

The only milk that dogs should consume is the milk of its own mother. However, there are certain plant based milks that are lactose free and are easily digestible for dogs and therefore safe used in moderation and it is best to buy organic if you can.

Almond Milk - Almond milk made from almonds is low in fat, but high in energy, proteins, lipids and fibre. It contains vitamins like calcium, iron, magnesium, phosphorus, potassium, sodium, and zinc. The other nutrients available in this milk include vitamins such as vitamin C, B-6, thiamine, riboflavin, niacin, folate and vitamin E.

Coconut Milk - Is creamy like whole milk. It has little protein, though, and about the same saturated fat as whole milk.

Hemp Milk - Thick and sometimes a little grainy. Made of hemp seeds which are high in heart-healthy omega-3 fatty acids. It also has protein but falls short in calcium.

Oat Milk - Oat milk is high in fibre, folic acid, vitamin E and phytochemicals. Oat milk is free of lactose and cholesterol and low in saturated fat.

Rice Milk - Rice milk is traditionally made from unsweetened brown rice. Free from cholesterol, saturated fat and lactose.

Soya Milk – One of the most common non dairy sources, soy milk is traditionally made from a mixture of soybeans and water. Soy milk is rich in calcium and protein and contains no saturated fat.

Flour

Flour is present in many pet food products and dogs actually do not need to consume flour at all. However, when baking treats for your dog it is important to use the right flour. Look for whole grain flour which uses the entire grain and therefore contains all the original nutrients. Again always try and buy organic where you can and try to buy local produce, because the addition of bleaching agents is not permitted in the UK.

Barley Flour - Barley flour contains gluten, the protein that helps baked goods rise, the type of gluten in barley flour does not promote adequate rising on its own, so barley flour is usually used with wheat flour. Look for whole grain barley flour, ground from hulled barley, not from pearl barley.

Brown Rice Flour – An excellent option for dogs that have food allergies and do not tolerate wheat.

Buckwheat Flour - Buckwheat flour is ideal for those avoiding wheat. Buckwheat is not a form of grain and does not contain gluten.

Chickpea Flour – Also known as Gram flour is high in protein, gluten free and non grain. Mixed with water is a popular alternative to egg replacement for vegan cooking.

Coconut Flour - low in carbohydrates, rich in fibre, protein and important nutrients. It makes a natural gluten-free grain-free alternative to wheat flour. Due to its high fibre content can improve the digestive system. Coconut flour is also extremely healthy, it's full of protein, fibre, has very little carbohydrate and fat, plus contains anti-microbial properties to aid in healthy gut function. Excellent as a thickener for doggie sauces and gravy.

Millet Flour - This flour is often used in combination with rice flour and other wheat free flours to provide extra protein and fibre.

Oat Flour – Oat flour has a naturally sweet nutty flavour, is high in protein and soluble fibre. Low in fat, wheat free, gluten free.

Quinoa Flour – The quinoa grain contains nutritious proteins, is high in fibre and gluten free.

Rice Flour – Milled from whole rice grains available either in white or brown flour. Rice flour is also good for baking, and it's a good alternative for dogs that are sensitive to wheat products.

Rye Flour – A great whole-grain flour for dogs because it is kinder on the digestive system, low in fat and controls insulin better than other popular flours, plus has more iron and calcium. The type of fibre in rye promotes a rapid feeling of fullness, so a good choice for using in treats for dogs trying to lose weight.

Spelt Flour – Spelt flour is a preferred choice to use instead of wheat flour because it is easier to digest, has a nutty flavour and has a good texture for baking. It is about 17% protein and contains a broad range of amino acids. Spelt protein does however include gluten and so should not be fed to celiac dogs.

Tapioca Flour - This flour has a slightly sweet flavour so is good to use in dog treat recipes. Plus tapioca flour is gluten free whilst also used to thicken sauces and make cakes when combined with other flours.

Wholemeal Flour - When it comes to baking, wheat flour is one of the most commonly used. However, some dogs are sensitive to wheat so if the dog you are baking for is wheat tolerant you can use it to bake treats. You can also use it in combination with different flours.

Wheat Gluten Flour (Vital) – Vital wheat gluten is specially milled wheat flour which is high in gluten and low in starch. Provides calcium, iron, potassium, sodium, phosphor, magnesium, Vitamins: A, Niacin, B1, B2, B6 and C. This flour is used as the main ingredient to make seitan, a meat alternative.

Herbs & Spices

Mother Nature has provided all we need to survive and by using traditional herbs and spices as medicine we are holistically healing the body by using these natural resources. Herbs and spices are rich in nutrients vital to the daily maintenance of your dog's health. Here are a few herbs and spices to get you inspired. Note: While certain herbs and spices do not create a hazard by themselves they can interfere with conventional western medicines, so if your dog is on medication seek a canine herbalist specialist before using.

Aloe Vera – Excellent for healing and soothing properties and decreases inflammation. Aloe Vera also has antibacterial, antifungal and antiviral properties. It also claims to help balance the immune system.

Alfalfa - Alfalfa is renowned as a cure for all inflammations, including arthritis. Alfalfa is also a blood purifier and bitter tonic, and contains the digestive enzyme betaine, which makes it a digestive aid as well. Alfalfa also contains a good supply of natural chlorophyll. Alfalfa is high in Vitamin A, Vitamin C, copper and niacin amongst many other minerals, making it a rich source of nutrients.

Aniseed – Great for daily health requirements such as brain function, Bone, ligament, tendon and muscle health, as well as cardiovascular health. Boosts the immune system and aids detoxification. Aniseed is a scent which dogs find irresistible, but also contains properties which help promote digestion, improve appetite and relieve flatulence.

Basil – Packed with vitamins A, B6, C, E and K. Two teaspoons of dried basil contains almost the same amount of calcium as a glass of milk.

Burdock - Burdock is most valuable for skin conditions and should be used over a long period of time to remove any systemic imbalance, which is often the cause. Burdock cleanses the blood and helps the body to detoxify, aids digestion and appetite. Burdock root is high in carbohydrates and insulin, and very high in iron, magnesium, silicon, thiamine, sodium, potassium, phosphorus and chromium.

Chamomile flowers– The calming & soothing herb can be added to home made treats and given before bedtime to dogs that are stressed or restless to help with a restful night's sleep.

Chickweed - Due to its high nutritional value it has been known to have a wide range of herbal benefits for maintaining optimal health, particularly with itchy skin.

Cinnamon - Ceylon cinnamon is an anti-oxidant, anti-inflammatory, anti-diabetic, and antiseptic, warming and soothing, calming, carminative (anti-flatulent). Cinnamon is said to have one of the highest antioxidant levels of all food sources. Cinnamon can help remove the alfatoxins present in foods. Cinnamon is also good for keeping teeth clean and fighting bad breath.

Dandelion – Mild diuretic herb helps to flush out toxins as well as high in anti-oxidants. Supports healthy function of the organs as well as keeping a healthy balance of microbial gut flora.

Echinacea - Echinacea is said to stimulate the part of the immune system that fights disease, bacteria and viruses, so a valuable herb to have around for wound healing and sick dogs.

Fennel seeds - Rich in dietary fibre, anti-oxidants vitamins and minerals. Fennel also helps protect the body from infection, disease and cancer. A fennel seed also help in the absorption of food to keep your dog's teeth clean and helping with digestion and has anti-inflammatory properties.

Ginseng - Ginseng is commonly prescribed to dogs. Ginseng has some very definite effects and may well help a dog with cancer and other aliments such as Addison's disease, congestive heart failure and diabetes, plus it can be used to minimise stress. Ginseng also contains anti-inflammatory saponins that can also help regulate cholesterol and blood sugar levels. Another component in ginseng root is geranium, which has a powerful hydrogenating effect on the body, especially the liver.

Kelp Seaweed – Has been scientifically proven to reduce dental plaque and tartar. Also aids poor hair growth and assists in the relief of rheumatic pain.

Lavender flowers – Natural calming and healing herb can be added to home made treats and given before bedtime to dogs that are stressed or restless to help with a restful night's sleep.

Marigold petals – A cleansing herb with natural source of lutein esters. Lutein is widely distributed in the body's tissues, and found as a colour pigment in the retina of healthy eyes where it acts as a shield against harmful light. Lutein is defined as a carotenoid vitamin, and it is related to beta-carotene and vitamin A. Canine studies show that lutein does play a role in enhancing immunity. Marigold petals have healing and antiseptic action for the skin.

Mint – Commonly known to help with oral health and bad breath but also has lots of other benefits too such as promotes digestion, eases nausea, aids in eliminating respiratory disorders.

Nettles – Source of vitamins and essential minerals. Nettle is a blood purifier, it can be a diuretic where there is excess fluid, it increases kidney and liver function and aids digestion. Nettles are high in calcium, chromium, magnesium, phosphorus, potassium, silicon, thiamine and Vitamin A. Nettle is also a catalyst for the absorption of many vitamins, minerals and trace minerals as well as several other herbs.

Oregano - Has been found to aid in the treatment of respiratory disease, arthritis, lyme and other tick borne diseases, while also providing immune system support. Plus oregano has the benefits of chlorophyll which can help control body odour, alleviate constipation and gas. Excellent when used as oil.

Parsley - Rich in anti-oxidants, vitamins and minerals which enhance the functioning of all organs, whilst helping the body pass toxins and fights bad breath.

Passion Flowers – Natural calming and healing herb can be added to home made treats and given before bedtime to dogs that are anxious or stressed to help with a restful night's sleep.

Rosehips - Well known as one of nature's richest sources of vitamin C it has been known to support the immune system, so helps with the absorption of essential minerals. Sometimes used as a natural support for joints.

Rosemary - Rich in vitamins, anti-oxidant, anti-inflammatory, anti fungal, and health promoting properties.

Spirulina – Contains unique phytonutrients that strengthens the immune system, has cleansing chlorophyll which helps detoxify and cleanse the body. Research has shown that Spirulina promotes good digestion and bowel function. Try giving your dog Spirulina and you will notice a shinier, more lustrous coat, fresher breath and better overall physical condition.

Turmeric - Turmeric is one of the most potent natural anti-inflammatory, aids digestion and helps support liver function, also aids the speed up of metabolism. Turmeric can also be used to treat bruises, inflammatory bowel disease, ulcers and is antiseptic. Turmeric can be used as a fresh grated root or added directly to food in small quantities.

Miscellaneous Ingredients

Apple cider vinegar – Apple cider vinegar aids digestive health, is good for allergies, bacterial infections, hot spots, ear infections, thinning fur and even parasites such as fleas, ringworm, ticks and fungus. ACV also has anti-inflammatory properties which help reduce muscle pain and inflammation whilst also balancing digestive enzymes in the body. A good remedy for food poisoning and digestive upsets such as intestinal gas and constipation. The important thing to remember is to buy organic, raw and unfiltered.

Couscous – Couscous is small pasta made of semolina, a form of wheat. Couscous provides a good source of lean vegetarian protein and is also rich in fibre. Good for diabetic dogs because it helps maintain sugar levels.

Nutritional yeast – Excellent source of protein and nucleotides. Nucleotides are the building blocks of DNA and RNA, just like amino acids are the building blocks of protein. Some dog food producers add nucleotides to their foods because they are beneficial to digestion, as well as developing a strong immune system and helps recovery after an injury. Contains unbeatable levels of B-vitamins as well as amino acids, protein, folic acid, biotin and minerals such as iron, magnesium, phosphorus, zinc, chromium, and selenium. Just sprinkle over meals for a nutty taste.

Peanut butter – Protein rich, antioxidants, vitamin E and manganese as well healthy fat. Ideally use home made.

Rice Noodles - Made from white rice flour, versatile and more delicate in texture and flavour than wheat based noodles such as pasta. Rice noodles are a low fat, gluten free food for dogs.

Seitan – Seitan is a high protein vegan 'meat' made from gluten flour. Dogs absolutely love it, and can be a great help when changing diets from a formerly carnivorous dog. But since wheat gluten should not be consumed to excess, seitan remains an occasional treat for dogs.

Sprouts - When seeds, grains and lentils sprout, an explosion of nutrients is released that would otherwise be unavailable for absorption by the canine digestive system. These nutrients can help optimise health and are easy to grow at home.

Spirulina - One of the most nutritious foods available. Spirulina eases the passage of waste through the digestive system, thereby reducing stress on the entire system. It also promotes healthy bacteria in the digestive system, and helps to improve the absorption of dietary nutrients. Animal based research suggests that spirulina may help to strengthen the immune system, improve gastrointestinal health, aid in detoxification, reduce the rate of cancer and help allergies.

Pasta - Dried pasta is made from a mixture of water and refined durum wheat or semolina. Whole grain pasta contains fewer calories and supplies around three times as much fibre and 25 percent more protein than traditional pasta. Pasta comes in all shapes and sizes and dogs in general love it. Pasta provides glucose, the crucial fuel for the brain and muscles. Pasta is an excellent source of complex carbohydrates, which provide a slow release of energy.

Tahini - Unshelled organic tahini is best as it's made from the whole sesame seed, leaving its nutritional value intact. High in vitamin E as well as B1, B2, B3, B5, B6, B15. Tahini is also high in minerals such as magnesium, potassium, iron, and phosphorus, and is an excellent source of calcium.

Tempeh - Tempeh is known for its high level of protein which is highly digestible as the result of the fermentation process. It contains B vitamins, minerals and is free of any cholesterol. Tempeh differs from tofu in that it contains more fibre because the whole soybean is used. In addition it contains phytochemicals such as isoflavones and saponins.

Tofu - Tofu, made from soybean curds, is naturally gluten-free and low calorie, contains no cholesterol and is an excellent source of protein, iron, and calcium. Tofu contains high levels of Tryptophan and relatively low levels of Tyrosin, making it a protein which supports the build up of Serotonin levels. Make your own scrambled tofu.

Whole wheat Biscuits – Home made wheat biscuits are good but you can also buy other well known brands if you do not have the time to bake them.

Yeast extract with added B12, no salt – Adds flavouring to stock, stews and gravies. The high B-Vitamin count in yeast extract is important for a healthy immune system, nervous system and maintaining energy levels. It also contains high levels of protein, great for maintaining healthy muscles.

SUPPLEMENTS

Supplement or not to supplement that is the question!

This is another controversial topic and not just in the vegan dog world but in general overall canine health opinions. I felt it a really important chapter to add because many people feel the need to supplement their dogs' diet and not just because their dogs are not consuming animal products. I believe it is important that where dogs are not in the best of health, supplements can be an important part of their lifestyle to help aid good health.

I believe that supplementing a healthy dog is detrimental to their health and a good balanced diet over a period of time is the best form of preventative medicine. Even a complete and balanced commercial dog food may contain quite a variety of different levels of nutrients. For example if you always feed the same food, any nutritional deficiencies or excesses present in that food will affect your dog over time. The same is true if you feed different varieties made by the same dog food company, since they tend to use the same vitamin and mineral formulations in all of their products. So therefore, if you choose to feed your dog the same commercial dog food you will probably have to use synthetic supplements at some point.

There are many different types of supplements: whole foods and synthetics; vitamins and minerals; essential fatty acids; green blends; digestive aids; and or combinations of these. Some nutritional guides will say the best supplements for your dog will depend on the diet you feed and your dog's overall health, which is quite right. However, when you look into further evidence whilst others have been part of mainstream canine diets for so long no one seems to challenge them. Generally anything new to us in life we have a hard time trying to come to terms that there might actually be another way of thinking because we have been conditioned to think otherwise. Healthy dogs benefit from a home made diet and fresh organic foods supply nutrients in their natural form, whole and complete. Evidence and research into synthetic supplements is another confusing roller coaster for many people. You can also give vitamin/mineral supplements, again do your research and if in doubt leave it out. I also recommend that you seek a qualified holistic veterinarian for help and further nutritional advice. Supplements should be used in conjunction with an optimum diet tailored to suit the healing needs of the individual dog and not to be used as a substitute for food.

There is no doubt that a quality diet extends the lifespan of dogs. However, breeding determines to a large degree on health and longevity. Sadly due to generations of bad breeding practices pedigree dogs have numerous genetic health conditions, some of which may lead to food allergies. Many manufactured dog foods contain dyes and colourings and seasonings. Also, many dog snacks and treats contain preservatives, since they are made out of such poor quality ingredients, that without a preservative they might become toxic.

Protein is present in every cell within the canine physical structure, it plays an important role in the body's ability to grow, stay healthy and repair itself. Food heals the body and dogs fed a plant based lifestyle without chemical additives are less likely to have skin aliments, ear infections, immune diseases, diabetes, cancer and behaviour problems; all these equals less visits to the veterinarian. So basically, spending money on quality ingredients will save you money in the long run. Dogs can absorb all the nutritional requirements quite adequately with a plant based lifestyle because they can source or synthesize all the nutrients they require from plant foods. However, many dog guardians choose to use Vegedog™ a supplement from James Peden's company, Harbingers of a New Age, which is a vegan/vegetarian dog food supplement for use in home made dog food, which I highly recommend.

Taurine is not considered a dietary requirement for dogs, but research indicates that some dogs may benefit. Many vegetarian and vegan pet food companies have now started to supplement their products with taurine as well as L-Carnitine. You can find more information about supplements in the reading and research section at the end of this book.

Taurine is a naturally occurring b-amino acid which is an essential dietary constituent for cats but a non-essential nutrient for dogs because they can readily synthesise it from the sulphur-containing amino acids (methionine and cysteine) which are found in nuts, spirulina and soybeans. Even when it is not found in abundance in a dog's diet, it is reported that dogs can readily produce their own and therefore it is a non essential nutrient to add to a *healthy* dogs diet. However, studies have shown taurine supplementation can help in the treatment of heart problems in dogs and some commercial dog foods now are found to contain taurine labelled as a health supplement. Healthy dogs synthesise sufficient taurine from dietary sulphur-containing amino acids such as methionine and cysteine as previously mentioned. Nevertheless, low plasma or low whole-blood taurine levels may be seen in dogs fed non-supplemented, very low protein diets, or foods that are low in sulphur-containing amino acids, or with poor availability of the sulphur-containing amino acids. It is always worth obtaining an annual health screen blood test which assists to establish baseline values, enabling your veterinarian to react to any changes before your pet becomes ill. This simple and inexpensive blood test can show changes characteristic of conditions such as diabetes, liver disease, kidney disease, anaemia and more, but will also confirm if your dog is healthy.

L-Carnitine a naturally occurring water-soluble vitamin is found as a component of all animal cells and only very small amounts are found in plants, which is why many dog guardians choose to supplement. Many people with dogs that have been diagnosed with congestive heart disease find supplementing with L-carnitine and taurine together have discontinued the conventional cardiovascular drug therapy with great results. According to research vegan dogs could benefit with L-carnitine and taurine, which are not generally added to commercial dog foods but added to some vegan commercial dog foods. Some suggest a deficiency of these nutrients may cause dilated cardiomyopathy, a condition in which the heart becomes large and flabby and can no longer function. This illness generally strikes large breeds when fed diets limiting in cysteine and methionine, suggesting that large breeds have a higher requirement for these sulphur amino acids compared to smaller breeds. Whilst these studies are inconclusive I find it difficult to understand that if L-carnitine and taurine are so crucial to the canine diet then why do manufacturers not include them? According to opinions supplementation is the only way to find out if your dog is deficient in these two amino acids because there is no conclusive test without a biopsy of the heart tissue. Many people conclude that their dogs' overall health has improved after supplementing L-carnitine and or taurine. It would be a recommendation to speak with a homoeopathic veterinarian to discuss supplementation to your dogs' diet before adding either to their daily routine because if your dog is healthy then these may not be required. Supplemental L-carnitine and taurine can be bought online but I have added more information about these two amino acids in the reading resources section at the back of this book to allow you to research further and make the decision for yourself.

Fresh, raw foods contain the highest level of enzymes and these enzymes assist in digestion. Cooked foods and dry convenient diets have been de-natured and are devoid of important enzymes: life-promoting elements. While they may maintain life they do not promote optimum health or longevity. Food enzymes are very sensitive and are easily destroyed by low moist heat (105-118 degrees F). Dry heat around 150 degrees F. Internal enzymes are damaged by factors, such as chlorine in drinking water, certain medicines, air pollution and chemical additives.

VITAMIN, MINERAL AND MICRO MINERAL TABLE

To ensure your dog is always on top form, feed quality nutritional food and supplement whenever you feel necessary. Older animals tend to absorb fewer vitamins, minerals, and electrolytes through the intestinal tract, and lose more of them through the kidneys and urinary tract. Also, some older animals eat less (due to conditions such as oral disease) and may not receive their daily needs of vitamins and minerals. Some evidence in dogs suggests that antioxidants such as vitamins A, E, and C (beta-carotene) may play a role in protecting against some normal ageing processes. Speak with a qualified canine nutritionist if you have any concerns and to determine which supplements may be beneficial for your dog.
In my opinion not enough research has been conducted on vitamins, minerals and supplements for animals to be able to be conclusive. However, dogs do require specific vitamins and minerals in their diet, whilst they can also be toxic in excess amounts. The table below illustrates the vitamin & mineral benefits and signs of deficiency and food rich sources.

Vitamin A
Benefits - Important for eyesight and growth, assist with cell reproduction and also stimulates immunity.
Deficiency may lead to poor eyesight, itchy eyes and skin.
Vitamin A rich foods are carrots, spinach, sweet potato, kale, peas, cabbage, butternut squash, dried apricots, cantaloupe melon and mango.

The B- Complex
Necessary for a healthy nervous system and said to be a natural flea repellent. Aids absorption of nutrients throughout the body (fats, protein and carbohydrates). Vitamin B complex consists of a multitude of B vitamins and will help your dog stay healthy and young and will allow him to deal with daily environmental stresses. B-complex vitamins can also be added as a supplement both to commercial and home made diets.

B-1 (Thiamine)
Benefits – Helps convert glucose into energy in nerves and muscles.
Deficiency may lead to fatigue, bloodshot eyes and depression.
B-1 Rich foods are brown rice, sunflower seeds, barley, oats, brewers yeast, lentils, wholemeal bread.

B-2 (Riboflavin)
Benefits – Necessary for red blood cell formation, helping convert food into energy, repairing body tissues.
Deficiency may lead to bloodshot eyes, light sensitivity, insomnia.
B-2 rich foods are green leafy vegetables, brewers yeast and spinach.

B-3 (Niacin)
Benefits – is said to help control seizures and reduce behaviour problems. Improves circulation whilst aiding the CNS (central nervous system) function and reduces cholesterol levels.
Deficiency may lead to the tongue turning black. Loss of appetite, inflamed gums and diarrhoea
B-3 rich foods are sunflower seeds, peanuts, brown rice and peas.

B-5 (Pantothenic Acid)
Benefits – Essential for stabilising the immune system and adrenal function. Important in fighting infections, allergies and inflammations.
Deficiency may lead to allergies or infections, depression, anxiety, hair loss, diarrhoea, premature greying.
B-5 rich foods include sunflower seeds and sweet potatoes.

B-6 (Pyridoxine)
Benefits – Essential for the metabolism of protein. Required for a healthy nervous system, red blood cell production as well as good brain function. B6 plays a role in the creation of antibodies in the immune system.
Deficiency may lead to anaemia, poor growth and skin lesions
B-6 foods include banana, dates, pineapple, watermelon, brussels sprouts, broccoli, butternut squash, sweet potato, brown rice, spinach, kidney beans and soy beans.

B-9 (Folate / Folic Acid)
Benefits - Folate occurs naturally in fresh foods, whereas folic acid is the synthetic form found in supplements. Supports red blood cell production and helps prevent anaemia. Folate is required for numerous body functions including DNA synthesis and repair, cell division, and cell growth.
Deficiency may lead to birth defects, hyperplasia of bone marrow, anaemia as well as decreased immune function.
B-9 foods include lentils, beans, spinach, lettuce, asparagus, broccoli, mango, whole wheat bread,

B-12 (Cobalamin)

Like the other B vitamins, it is involved in energy metabolism and other related biological processes. Prevents nerve damage and promotes normal growth and development. Necessary for normal digestion and natural food absorption. Vitamin B12 helps maintain the good health and increases immunity as well as strong bones and muscles.
Deficiency may lead to lethargy, anaemia, lack of appetite.
Vitamin B12 is the one vitamin that is available from meat sources in food so it is essential that you add nutritional yeast with added B-12 to home cooked meals or use a synthetic supplement.

Biotin – B-Complex
Biotin is a B-complex vitamin that has been identified as a necessary nutrient for a century, but has only begun to be understood in the past two decades. It has also been previously referred to as co-enzyme R, vitamin H, and vitamin B7, with the different names adding to the confusion surrounding its role in normal metabolism. Essential for thyroid and adrenal health, building a strong nervous system and is said to cure coprophagia.
Deficiency may lead to hair loss, skin disorders and diarrhoea.
Biotin rich foods are sweet potato, carrots, oats, tomatoes, peanuts, soy beans and corn.

Vitamin C
Benefits – An antioxidant, fights pollution, cleans toxins from the blood and tissues. Dogs produce their own vitamin C which is synthesized in the liver of healthy dogs, which helps protect the body from lead toxicity, keeps teeth strong and retards the ageing process.
Lack of – May lead to muscle and joint weakness, loosening of teeth, haemorrhages.
Vitamin C rich foods are brussels sprouts, parsley, kale, broccoli, bell peppers, dark green leafy Vegetables, strawberries, broccoli, mange tout, pineapple and tahini.

Vitamin D
Benefits - known as the "sunshine vitamin" since it is manufactured by the body after being exposed to sunshine. Vitamin D is vital to the body as it promotes absorption of calcium and magnesium, bone development, control of cell growth, neuromuscular functioning, immune functioning, and alleviation of inflammation, which are essential for the normal development of healthy teeth and bones. It also helps maintain adequate levels of calcium and phosphorus in the blood.
Lack of vitamin D may lead to a bone deficiency called rickets. Dietary deficiency of vitamin D is substantial, research suggests that low blood levels

of vitamin D are associated with poor survival, especially Dogs with congestive heart failure (CHF).

Vitamin E

Benefits - plays a significant role as an antioxidant which protects body tissue from the damage of oxidation. Important in the formation of red blood cells and the use of vitamin K. Slows down the ageing process, prevents cataracts, boosts the immune system, protects the body against pollutants and heals the skin.
Deficiency may lead to muscle wastage, eye problems such as retinal degradation, impaired immune system and reduced fertility.
Vitamin E rich foods are silken tofu, cooked spinach, sunflower seeds, cooked butternut squash, cooked broccoli, peanuts.

Vitamin K - Phytonadione

Benefits - Dogs produce their own vitamin K which is synthesized in the body of healthy dogs, which helps control blood clotting.
Deficiency may affect the functioning of the liver, one of the primary sites for synthesizing the enzymes necessary for coagulation. Increased clotting time and haemorrhage.
Vitamin K rich foods are green leafy vegetables, beans, cooked brussels sprouts, cucumber, cauliflower, kale.

Calcium

Benefits – Essential for bone, muscle and teeth growth, blood coagulation, muscle contraction, and nerve impulse transmission.
According to studies calcium and phosphorous need to be in balance in the body to maintain the growth and structure of the skeletal system and vitamin D is required to activate calcium.
Deficiency may lead to nervousness, lameness, muscle spasms, heart palpitations, osteoporosis and increased cholesterol levels. Calcium deficiencies may be brought on by high meat diets because meat contains unbalanced amounts of phosphorous.
Calcium rich foods are tofu, sesame seeds, spinach, dark leafy greens, broccoli,

Choline

Benefits – Choline is an essential nutrient for brain health, intelligence and synaptic plasticity. The body uses choline for a variety of functions that benefit not only the brain, but also helps the body maintain water balance whilst helping to control cell growth. According to studies regular choline supplementation may help prevent or treat canine cognitive disorder. Most

importantly for ageing dogs choline produces the major nerve transmitter acetylcholine, a neurotransmitter chiefly important for memory
Deficiency may lead to loss of body weight, an increase in fat in the liver.
Choline rich foods are tofu, soy, flaxseeds, brussels spouts, broccoli, oregano, green beans, peas, cabbage.

Iron
Benefits – Required in the production of haemoglobin, enzyme function, immune support and energy.
Deficiency may lead to anaemia, lethargy, pale gums and decreased growth rate.
Iron rich foods are chickpeas, soybeans, lentils, spinach, tahini, kidney beans, nutritional yeast, kelp, green leafy vegetables and dried dates.

Magnesium
Benefits – helps detoxify the body from lead and metal poisoning. Helps with formation of bone and teeth, maintains a healthy heart and assists the absorption of calcium and potassium and therefore important for enzyme function and the nervous system.
Deficiency may lead to high blood pressure, seizures, muscle spasms , bone pain and hyper irritability, and depression
Magnesium rich foods are pumpkin seeds, spinach, whole grains, leafy green vegetables, soy beans, bananas.

Manganese
Required for normal reproduction, bone and cartilage growth and is necessary for enzyme activity and collagen growth.
Deficiency may lead to poor bone formation and stiffness but studies have shown that eating a plant based diet tends to be a rich source of manganese.
Manganese rich foods include oats, brown rice, kale, spinach, butter beans, pumpkin seeds, peas, beetroot, leafy green vegetables.

Potassium and Sodium
Working together these two minerals help to maintain fluid balance in the cells in the body, as well as muscle functions, transmission of nerve impulses, heart activity and the production of hydrochloric acid in the stomach.
Deficiency may lead to dehydration, restlessness, muscular paralysis, poor growth and prolonged diarrhoea and vomiting. Potassium deficiency in dogs is often due to an excessive loss of potassium rather than too little dietary intake.
Potassium and Sodium rich foods include bananas, sweet potatoes, squash, pinto beans, lentils, dried apricots and dates, red tomatoes. An excellent source of potassium replacement is apple cider vinegar.

Selenium
Selenium is required by the body for functioning the thyroid gland and may help protect against free radical damage and cancer. Selenium is a trace mineral which was ironically recognised as a toxic substance before it was identified as a necessary nutrient for dogs but in low amounts as an antioxidant.
Deficiency is very rare in dogs, but may lead to immune deficiencies, muscle weakness and skin problems.
Selenium rich foods include sunflower seeds, whole grains and green vegetables.

Silicon
Silicon helps the body heal itself supporting the immune system whilst keeping bones and cartilage healthy.
Deficiency may lead to bone and joint conditions. Dogs that eat a large amount of grass have been found to have silicon deficiency.
Silicon rich foods include green leafy vegetables, whole grains, beetroot, alfalfa and flaxseeds.

Zinc
Benefits - Necessary for healing tissues, wounds and the utilisation of copper, B complex vitamins, vitamin A, calcium and phosphorus.
Deficiencies may lead to immune system diseases, skin problems and allergic reactions.
Zinc rich foods include pumpkin seeds, sesame seeds, lentils and quinoa.

Although the evidence on supplements is quite straight forward, if you feed your dog nutritionally balanced meals and he is energetic and fit, his body probably doesn't require supplements. But if you think he isn't getting enough nutrition from his food, supplements can be helpful. Keep in mind that minerals especially should never be given to puppies unless prescribed by a veterinarian or a canine nutritionist. For example, Calcium is good for human bones but it actually prevents bone formation and can damage maturing joints and cartilage in puppies, as well as too much zinc can be toxic. Supplements can interact with or hinder absorption of vital nutrients in foods sources or reduce the effectiveness of prescribed medications. If you feel that your dog is lethargic, sluggish, his fur is dull, has dandruff, coprophagia or if the sclera of the eye is not white, then these could well be signs of a vitamin deficiency. Always seek advice from a professional holistic canine nutritionist if your dog becomes symptomatic or if you suspect a deficiency in the diet before administering synthetic supplements.

Digestive enzymes

Grated raw carrots, beetroot, sprouted lentils and barley grass powder are examples of good sources of enzymes and fibre. It is important to add raw food into your dogs' meals, or as treats, as these are particularly essential for vitality. Some people recommend adding digestive enzymes to dogs' meals and many suggest the particular kind that dogs need are: Amylase, Protease, Lipase, Cellulase and Lactase. *Harbinger's of a New Age* sells Prozyme; an enzyme supplement for dogs containing these enzymes. However, not all digestive enzyme supplements are helpful. I believe that some digestive enzymes will help your dog, whilst some will do very little and others may actually harm the health of your dog. Again it is always good to do your own research. It is a hard decision to use synthetic supplements but one can only go by the health of your dog. I have my dogs' blood value taken yearly to make sure they are not deficient in anything, as well as a Titer test to make sure that their antibodies are healthy. Personally I find this is the most conclusive way of knowing the health of my dogs because if you were to supplement year in year out you never know whether your dog actually needs the additional supplements, when they can do a lot more harm than good. However, if any of my dogs were found to be deficient in any vitamin or mineral I would have no hesitation to use a vegan synthetic supplement if they couldn't be derived from natural ingredients.

WAYS TO HELP YOUR DOG ACHIEVE LONGEVITY

Several factors can influence the lifespan of your canine friend. I believe these are in order of good breeding genes, food, exercise, stress levels, rest and love. I have written a few guidelines that may help along the way.

Good Breeding Genetics is crucial if you are to achieve longevity with your canine friend. Whilst this is not always possible in today's society because many puppies are bred by battery farms, backyard or hobby breeders where they have been bred purely for monetary gain. A responsible breeder will always health test their breeding dogs for breed specific health conditions, they will also hand rear the pups themselves and forge a socialisation plan whilst the dam plays her important motherly role in making sure the pups get the nutrients from her milk, her warmth and her knowledge, together with learning from it's litter-mates. Sadly pups that have been bred in battery farms will not have this start in life and many will not even survive. When choosing a dog to join your family it is a very personal choice but the morally responsible way to do so is by rescuing and to support your local rescue centre.

Food which we have already discussed is a very important life tool. We now know that dogs flourish eating fresh nutritious foods, much like ourselves. The first twelve months of a pups life is the most important stage so it is very important for them to have the best start and everything that you do during this time will have a huge effect on the rest of their life.

Socialisation is fundamental to be able to walk your dog in everyday situations. Introducing your dog to as many new experiences as possible will help him become accustomed to the world and your routine; this allows him to be well balanced and happy. Sharing new experiences together and making them fun will make a lifelong bonding relationship and in turn bring out his true personality and the dog he will become.

Exercise and fresh air is an essential part of your daily routine and is a key contributor to health, vitality and aid the longevity of your dog. It is more comfortable for your dog to wear a harness rather than a collar because the throat is a very sensitive and vulnerable part of the dogs anatomy and one that is overlooked by many dog guardians. Collars can exacerbate many conditions causing suffering, including crushing of the trachea with partial or complete asphyxiation and crushing of, and sometimes fracture of, the bones in the larynx. The most comfortable way to walk your dog is by investing in a well designed to fit fleece lined harness. Do your homework when researching a harness, there are many on the market and it is always good to get recommendations. It is important to remember that exercising your dog on a full stomach, directly before or after a meal is extremely dangerous, especially with large, deep chested breeds which are prone to Gastric Dilation Volvulus syndrome (GDV), also known as bloat or gastric (stomach) torsion, where the stomach dilates and then rotates, or twists, and should be considered a life threatening emergency when it occurs. Dogs can die of bloat within several hours so if you see any symptoms such as a swollen stomach, non productive vomiting or retching it is advisable to visit your veterinary clinic immediately. Dogs should not be exercised within 1 hour before it is fed, or 2-3 hours after it has been fed. I believe it is extremely important that dogs should be allowed to have access to free runs every day to be able to learn and express their natural instincts. A variation of walks every day is also vital to allow new smells and to offer a wealth of learning behaviours with other dogs. Sadly in the UK today it is very difficult to find large open spaces unless you are lucky enough to live in a rural or coastal setting. The quality and quantity of exercise needed will vary as your dog ages or experiences periods of weight change or convalescence, so it is important to bear in mind that the exercise needs of your canine companion are subject to change. Exercise allows freedom to express normal behaviour and to allow his true personalities to shine through.

Play is important to stimulate the brain for mental health. The link between mental and physical changes involved with the ageing process is not proven between brain and body. However, we do know the hypothalamus in the brain helps control the endocrine system which sends chemical messengers around the body. Exercising the dog's mind by stimulating senses delays natural deterioration of ageing and senility. Changes in the brain resulting from senility can lead to one or more of the following symptoms; loss of house training, lack of interest in food and attention, circling and compulsive behaviours such as paw licking, inappropriate barking and whining, weakness, tremors, changes in sleep patterns and pacing at night, 'forgetfulness' and a decrease in awareness of surroundings. Play is important for mental stimulation at any age but the aged dog benefits immensely from this. Environments that encourage exercise, mental stimulation and play situations help minimise mental decline. Although the ageing process is probably under the control of a hormonal biological clock, dogs that have an enriched environment, together with a nutritional diet, show the best learning results and is key to a healthy, happy and long life.

Games depending on the age and capability, mental stimulation should be daily however short or long, your dog will decide. As well as retrieving toys there are many brain training games available on the market, such as puzzles, toys, treat dispensing toys. The main key factor here is to interest the canine and encourage with a suitable activity to fit in to your daily routine. Older dogs' reflexes are slower so 1 toy at a time will be less confusing. Play stimulates inventiveness, teaches problem solving and creates social bonding. Reinforce good behavior and cues with a tasty treat.

Agility is an obstacle course for dogs which is another good way for humans to use this natural behaviour and fly-ball is another great activity. Physical stimulation is very difficult to advise without the knowledge of age, background and health history. The main key advice is to do as much or as little as the canine is capable of and of course happy to do, keeping the amount of daily exercise fairly constant, as unusually strenuous activity may make the dog sore or ache the next day. Little and often about 20-30 minutes twice a day, do not take the dog out if he is lame, stiff or in pain. Providing a comfortable bed / den will allow him to relax at the end of the day.

Grooming is a great way of bonding with your dog as well as making sure that their skin and coat is in tip top condition. Touch and massage is a great tool to ensure that there are no lumps & bumps on the body.

Freedom to express normal behaviour and allowing your dog the freedom to run and roam in a safe environment is essential for them to explore the world in their own time, whilst allowing them to feel free; this also helps with achieving independence which is very important. Left to their own devices dogs would chase and run for hours on end. Chasing prey is inbuilt and as natural to a dog as eating. Without this vital impulse, dogs in the wild would never have had a chance at survival. However, as dogs now live in a human driven world they no longer have to chase prey to provide food for their pack, but their instincts still remain intact.

Stress Levels can significantly make a dog break down mentally and physically. I have seen many broken dogs over the years and this has been brought on by stress. Stress by being kept in solitary confinement, stress by being used as a play toy by children, stress of being misunderstood by guardians leaving the house all day and leaving the dog to its own devices.

Rest is very important to dogs. If dogs were allowed to be free they would spend around 14 hours a day resting. Resting is the body's way of regenerating cells and resting the body organs. Rest allows an exercised and mentally stimulated dog to experience the pleasurable chemicals within the brain, which promote a calm and relaxed and sometimes euphoric feeling. I would imagine dogs probably feel much the same way we humans do after a great workout. Make a safe haven for your dog in the way of a den like structure. Make this comfortable with blankets and his favorite toys. Keep the door open if you have a crate to allow him to come and go as he pleases when you are at home. Always make sure your dog has access to fresh water.

Love may sound very simple but this is a very powerful attribute of achieving longevity. Love means that you give your soul and passion to that one being. This means you will protect it, nurture it and as your dog enters their twilight years the changes mentally and physically again greatly depends on breeding and I believe also depends on the guardian. A guardian who has a relaxed energetic manner that has a set routine will ultimately instill happiness and calmness. New experiences are crucial for achieving good behavior and eliminating fear. If your dog has a negative experience, take him back but next time make it more positive, reward good behaviour with treats and lots of praise. Healthy active dogs will have a slower senile change to the brain than unhealthy and inactive ones.

'My little dog — a heartbeat at my feet. – **Edith Wharton'**

ABOUT THE AUTHOR

I have read and studied scientific resources regarding canine nutrition for many years working in canine psychology and animal welfare. What I have learnt from my studies into nutrition is that my canine friends have never been happier and healthier living on a plant based diet; they have had fewer visits to the veterinarian clinic, their coats shine, they have more energy, no more bad breath and their general well being has quite frankly been an amazing transformation. The proof simply speaks for itself, they are the healthiest and happiest they have ever been.

I was raised as a meat eater but became vegetarian around the age of 13 when I matured enough to realise that I couldn't possibly face eating animals. I had great empathy for animals and saw them as my friends; not to mention they were fluffy and cute! I can remember very clearly that we had a pet rabbit called Suzie that sadly passed away in the night. Over the subsequent days we had rabbit stew for dinner one evening. I couldn't get my head around the fact that it might be Suzie our beloved pet rabbit that I was eating and even though my parents told me that it was a 'wild' rabbit and not our 'pet' rabbit I still could not differentiate between the two. Why would the same animal have a different outcome in life just because we chose to name it a pet? How could I have not seen the truth before? And more importantly why hadn't anyone told me? Why wasn't this taught to me at school? Why were people hiding the truth? And why do the majority of humans feel superior to animals and what gives us the right to take the life of another sentient being that wants to live? So many questions but not many answers in those days...So from that day forward I haven't eaten meat. Then when I was in my 30's I had an epiphany when I suddenly realised I wasn't actually making as much difference to the cruelty, exploitation and suffering that animals endure after all, when a vegan friend educated me about the cruelty of dairy farming. How the cow endures year after year of being artificially inseminated, her offspring taken away at just a few minutes old only to be whisked away for the veal industry, often travelling hundreds of miles to their destination to be kept in solitude for just a few months before being brutally killed for human consumption. Its mother has an average lifespan of just 5 years living as a dairy cow, that's 15 years she will miss off her natural lifespan just to produce milk which was designed for her babies and her babies alone. Much more came to light in relation to other aspects of veganism such as daily household and cleaning products that we use within the home and personal products such as hair shampoo, make up and the cruelty that laboratory animals have to suffer to test these products. It is estimated that every 10 seconds a laboratory animal dies in the UK, and yes some of them are dogs. I haven't written this book to preach about veganism, but wanted to share my experiences and knowledge in the hope that it might touch on the consciousness of a few people which in turn may save lives. I know that I would have lived a vegan lifestyle many years ago if there was more education and awareness of the cruelty suffered, not just in battery farms and slaughter houses, but literally every where you turn there it is, cruelty and exploitation of our sentient friends. It doesn't have to be this way; Mother Nature has kindly provided us with nutritious delicious foods which allow our bodies to thrive and heal from within.

Once a fully fledged vegan, I started to speak with other like minded people to discuss various issues that one may come across. Then one day a fellow vegan asked me what I fed my dogs; I replied 'oh they have a wonderful diet of fish and fresh vegetables'. She replied, 'so you don't wish to eat sentient beings yourself but you don't want to pass this moment of light onto your beloved canine friends you love so much?' Hmm this was a quandary indeed. As a canine psychologist I have always been very mindset that dogs are omnivores not carnivores, but can they really thrive on a plant based diet? From that moment I decided to research vegan nutrition and have since discovered another vegan world to which I have been dedicated to ever since. Since that empowering light bulb moment my canine friends have been vegan and have flourished health wise in every way and I am happy in the knowledge that no animal had to suffer in order for us to live and that is truly the most wonderful feeling.

This book gives you, the reader, some information to ponder on and also some recipes that you can try and incorporate into your dog's lifestyle. Even if you feed them a nutritious plant based meal once or twice a week, or just add a small portion into their daily meals, you will soon notice that your dog will crave the vegetables and nutrients he needs, whilst showing many health benefits along the way. Whilst this is the first edition, there will be many more to follow with more information and more recipes to keep your canine friends healthy and happy with a variety of delicious foods.

Veganism can be a lonely path to take if you do it alone because, sadly, many people believe that it is extreme. The only thing *extreme* about veganism is that we are all *extremely* passionate about animals, humanity and the planet. I believe that all animals have a soul and those who do not see this have obviously never truly been in the company of animals. If you actually look, really look at an animal, you can see an aura around them, for they are extremely intuitive and spiritual, they know more than we ever will and it is our duty to protect them.

Think occasionally of the suffering of which you spare yourself the sight -
Albert Schweitzer

RESOURCES

Vegan Dog Food Manufacturers

Amì - An Italian brand inspired by the original Italian creativity and the well-known worldwide 'Made in Italy' quality for food. Amì is 100% vegan, 100% Italian and 100% pro-active - www.amipetfood.com

Benevo - An independent UK based producer of complete vegetarian and vegan pet foods, treats and accessories - www.benevo.com

V-dog - Recognised as the original vegetarian dog food. First produced in 1980, the range of three wholesome, natural and meat-free feeds consists of Crunchy Nuggets, Traditional Flakes and Wheat Gluten Free Mixer - www.v-dog.co.uk

Yarrah - A Dutch Company, founded in 1992. Back then, organic pet food was not produced yet, so Yarrah was the first company to start producing organic dog –and later on- cat food - www.yarrah.com

Suppliers of Vegan Dog Products (UK)

Dorwest Herbs, veterinary herbal medicine - www.dorwest.com

Ethical Pet Store - www.ethical-pets.co.uk

Helios Homeopathic Remedies - www.helios.co.uk

Veggie Pets - www.veggiepets.com

Woof and Brew, herbal tea for dogs - www.woofandbrew.com

Research Your Own Dog Food

Dog Food Analysis - www.dogfoodanalysis.com

Food Advisor - www.dogfoodadvisor.com

Grain Free Living - www.grainfreeliving.com

Know Better Pet Food - www.knowbetterpetfood.com

Nutrition Data – www.nutritiondata.self.com

Pet Food Recall - www.petfoodrecall.org

Pet Education - www.peteducation.com

Pet Poison Advice - www.petpoisonhelpline.com

The Worlds Healthiest foods - www.whfoods.com

Veganism; The Truth Has Come – www.thevegantruth.blogspot.co.uk

Vegan Dog and Cat Nutrition – www.vegandogandcat.com

Vegan Dog Nutrition Association - www.vegandognutritionassociation.com

Vegetarian Dogs - www.vegetariandogs.com

Canine Health Website Resources

British Association of Homoeopathic Veterinary Surgeons, The (BAHVA) - www.bahvs.com

Canine Health Concern - www.canine-health-concern.org.uk

Dog Health Survey | Vegan dogs – http://spot.humaneresearch.org/content/dog-health-survey

Dogs Naturally Magazine - www.dogsnaturallymagazine.com

Dr. Alfred Plechner - www.drplechner.com

Indogo Plant Powdered Dogs - www.indogolife.com

L-Carnitine or Taurine Deficiency - www.carnitine-taurine.com

Pet Welfare Alliance - www.petwelfarealliance.org

Tellington TTouch - www.ttouch.com

Vegan Vet - www.veganvet.com

Worm Count - www.wormcount.com

Interesting Reading Resources

China Study, The - **Colin Campbell**

Dominion – **Matthew Scully**

Eating Animals by **Jonathan Safran Foer**

Eat Like You Care: An Examination of the Morality of Eating Animals - **Gary Francine**

Farmageddon: The True Cost of Cheap Meat - **Philip Lymbery**

Growl: Life Lessons, Hard Truths, and Bold Strategies from an Animal Advocate – **Kim Stallwood**

In Defence of Dogs: Why Dogs Need Our Understanding – **John Bradshaw**

Inside of a Dog: What Dogs See, Smell, and Know - **Alexandra Horowitz**

Natural Health for Dogs & Cats – **Dr Richard Pitcairn**

Natural Healing for Dogs & Cats – **Diane Stein**

Nutrient Requirements of Dogs and Cats - **National Research Council**

Obligate Carnivore – **Jed Gillen**

Prescription for Nutritional Healing – **James & Phyllis Balch**

Shock to the System: The Facts about Animal Vaccination, Pet Food and How to Keep Your Pets Healthy – **Catherine O'Driscoll**

The Protein Myth: Significantly Reducing the Risk of Cancer, Heart Disease, Stroke, and Diabetes While Saving the Animals and the Planet - **David Gerow Irving**

The Dog Crisis – **Iris Nowell**

Vegetarian Cats & Dogs – **James A. Peden**

Why Dogs Hump and Bees Get Depressed: The Fascinating Science of Animal Intelligence, Emotions, Friendship, and Conservation – **Marc Bekoff**

Educational and Ethical Websites

C.A.R.I.A.D. The Campaign To End Puppy Farming – www.cariadcampaign.co.uk

Compassion in World Farming - www.ciwf.org.uk

Free from Harm empowers consumers to dramatically reduce our impact on animals and ecosystems – www.freefromharm.org

Friends of The Earth - www.foe.co.uk

In the words of Dr. Elliot Katz, be a dog guardian not an owner. Take The Guardian Pledge today! - www.guardiancampaign.co.uk

Organic Consumers Association - www.organicconsumers.org

Pet Remedy Charts - www.petremedycharts.com

Peta; People for the Ethical Treatment of Animals - http://www.peta.org/living/companion-animals/vegetarian-cats-dogs

Population Matters - www.populationmatters.org

The Soil Association; the UK's leading membership charity campaigning for healthy, humane and sustainable food - www.soilassociation.org

Grow Your Own Organic Garden

Grow and save your own seeds - www.savingourseeds.org

Organic Garden - www.organicgardeninfo.com

Research and advice network- www.gardenorganic.org.uk

Research and promote vegan organic methods - www.veganorganic.net

The Dog-Scaped Yard eBook - www.moplants.com/ebooks

The Federation of City Farms & Community Gardens - www.farmgarden.org.uk

The National Allotment Society - www.nsalg.org.uk

The Royal Horticultural Society - www.rhs.org.uk

Wildflower seeds - www.wildflower.org.uk

What to eat and grow now – www.eatseasonably.co.uk

Non Animal Tested Companion Animal Foods | UK

Almo Nature - 020 3332 0087

Ami - 02392 45 33 55 (vegetarian/vegan food, available in the UK from www.veggiepets.com)

Antos Ltd - 0844 800 9201 (vegetarian dog snacks available)

Applaws Natural Cat & Dog Food - 08707 508606

Barker & Barker - 01253 811887 (includes vegetarian dog treats)

Barking Heads & Meowing Heads - 0808 100 8885

Benevo - 02392 45 33 55 (vegetarian/vegan food, available in the UK from Veggie Pets)

Burns Pet Nutrition Ltd - 01554 890482

Cambrian Pet Foods Ltd - 01559 384216

CLINIVET ® Nutrition - 028 9447 3840

The Co-operative Food Supermarket - 0800 0686 727

CSJ Specialist Canine Feeds - 01745 710470

Eden Holistic Pet Foods Ltd - 01782 322409

Europa Pet Foods - 0845 658 0987

Feelwell's - 0870 977 0044

Forthglade Ltd - 01837 83322

Fromm and Eagle Pack - 01531 633985

Haith's - 0800 298 7054 (bird food)

Healthy Paws - 0151 931 3336

Land of Holistic Pets Ltd - 0845 373 4120 (vegetarian dog food available)

Laughing Dog - 01788 810283

Lily's Kitchen - 0845 680 5459

Mariners Choice - 01472 867170

Mark and Chappell - 01582 583888

My Pet Foods - 01227 723816 (rabbit food)

Nature Diet - 01362 822320

Organipets - 0845 3880935

Pero Pet Foods - 0800 917 9697

Pets' Kitchen - 01285 711151

Pooch & Mutt - 020 8133 7667

Pure Pet Food Ltd - 020 3326 2970

Roger Skinner Limited - 01379 384 247

Supreme Petfoods Limited - 01473 823296 (food for rabbits and small animals)

The Dog Deli - 01603 860 896

Trophy Pet Foods - 01367 240333

V-Dog - 02392 45 33 55 (vegan food, available in the UK from www.veggiepets.com)

Vitalin Pet Foods - 01765 605156

Yarrah Organic Petfood - (organic food including vegetarian/vegan dog food which can be ordered in the UK from their website)

Recipe Notes:-

Recipe Notes:-

If you would like to contact me please email vegandoglifestyle@hotmail.com

Made in United States
North Haven, CT
03 May 2024